Commercial Awareness and Business Decision-Making Skills

How to understand and analyse company financial information

Paul Rodgers

AMSTERDAM • BOSTON • HEIDELBERG • LONDON
NEW YORK • OXFORD • PARIS • SAN DIEGO
SAN FRANCISCO • SINGAPORE • SYDNEY • TOKYO

CIMA Publishing is an imprint of Elsevier

CIMA Publishing is an imprint of Elsevier
Linacre House, Jordan Hill, Oxford OX2 8DP, UK
30 Corporate Drive, Suite 400, Burlington, MA 01803, USA

First edition 2007

British Library Cataloguing in Publication Data
A catalogue record for this book is available from the British Library

978 0 7506 8384 5

For information on all CIMA publications
visit our website at books.elsevier.com

Typeset by Integra Software Services Pvt. Ltd, Pondicherry, India
www.integra-india.com

Printed and bound in Great Britain

07 08 09 10 11   10 9 8 7 6 5 4 3 2 1

One's mind, once stretched by a new idea, never regains its original dimensions.

Oliver Wendell Holmes (1841–1935)

Contents

Introduction to the book

The chances are that if you have picked this book from the shelf at the local library or bookshop, you have a career in business or are considering this as a probable direction in the future. This should imply that you have some idea of the mechanics by which business works, but let us stand back for a moment and ask ourselves a few questions – the answers to be which might be rather uncomfortable!

Q: How do businesses interact, in a written format, with the world around them?

A: Invoices, credit notes, goods received notes and so on.
Marketing flyers, brochures
Overdue payment reminders
Financial statements

Q: When divisional directors prepare budgets for the period ahead what medium is used to subsequently compare actual with the budgets' predictions?

A: Monthly management accounts

Q: If you hold shares in a public company what is the main correspondence you receive in addition to notification of the annual general meeting and dividend tax vouchers?

A: Summary financial statements

The common theme is financial information, and yet the very thought may have you in a cold sweat. However, there is some good news as financial information can be viewed very differently from the perception it conveys to most.

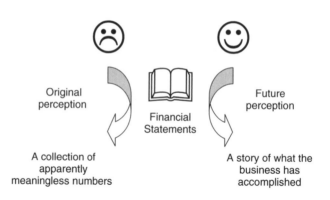

Original perception — Financial Statements — Future perception

A collection of apparently meaningless numbers

A story of what the business has accomplished

As with any good novel there is one possible constraint to our understanding, and that is it must be written in a language we comprehend. What follows is designed to act as your financial statement phrase book and dictionary rolled up into one. It will enable you to draw meaning from the wealth of information contained within financial documents that were previously considered out of bounds.

Furthermore, although the pages that follow will be an invaluable springboard to those starting out in the world of accountancy, its primary aim is to enable commercial managers working within every facet of a business to meet some clearly defined objectives:

1. Understand the impact of choices in accounting treatment upon the financial data an entity produces
2. Use tools to complement the financial data, and enable you to ask perceptive questions that elicit answers that would not otherwise be made available
3. Develop an approach that enables them to review previously unseen financial information efficiently and effectively
4. Add value within a commercial business environment.

This book is also designed to enable you to take commercial documents, and visualize how they interact with the work of an accountant. Effectively to understand how paperwork, or its electronic equivalent, with which you are familiar ultimately contribute to the accounting process. This will explain why every board of management appear to focus on financial data.

At this stage I am sure you are keen to get started – so dive in and let us make the numbers speak!

Why do Financial Statements Exist?

The expectation gap – do not believe first impressions

Imagine that a cross section of society have been gathered in a large room, and each participant asked to write down what they perceive as the purpose of financial statements. The answers would be many and varied with some claiming that they are an academic exercise with no bearing on the real world, others suggesting they are misleading because accountants are trained to 'always make it look better than it really is', and yet some claiming there must be something to it as all businesses seem fixated with numbers.

By contrast if the same room had been occupied by captains of industry, financial analysts and potentially most significantly the providers of finance the response would have been very different. The financial statements of an entity would be perceived as a key building block in understanding both the past performance of the business and its future prospects.

There is clearly a sizeable gap between the expectations of different groups and this has served to do financial statements a huge injustice. Dismissed as irrelevant or understood only by specialists with years of training appears to leave little middle ground.

The truth about financial statements is very different as the principles of accounting that underpin them are not a mystical art reserved for the few, but an easily grasped tool kit that opens the gateway to a wealth of useful information. Whether you are an experienced business manager with no previous accounting knowledge now being asked to review financial information or someone just starting out in business the 'accounts', as they are often known, offer a resource that should not be neglected.

Consequently, it is important to throw away any preconceptions you may have about financial statements as it is these which sustain the expectation gap. Start the journey with your mind as a clean sheet on which to record the good news about how surprisingly easy it is to understand and analyse financial information to the benefit of not only yourself but your business as well.

Let the journey begin . . .

The division of ownership and hands-on management

With the exception of small companies or incentive schemes offered to employees it is unusual for an investor in a business to be actively involved in its day-to-day management also. If this observation is combined with the fact that a company is a separate legal entity capable of signing contracts in its own name rather than that of the individuals of which it is comprised, then the primary need for financial information becomes apparent.

In Figure 1.1 an investor unrelated to the company has decided to make an investment in the shares of a company listed on a stock exchange. If these are new shares released by the company then uptake by investors will lead to an injection of cash flowing into the business to fund new and existing projects. The company may purchase new machinery or recruit additional skilled staff, but the contracts involved will be in the name of the company and not the investor who originally provided the money.

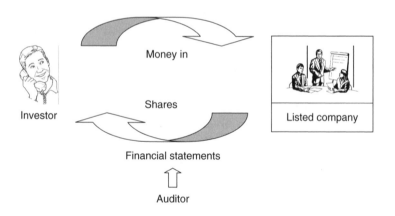

Figure 1.1 The division of ownership and control

This detachment between the investor and the company is known as the veil of incorporation, and could result in the investor feeling very alienated as they would be unaware of the purpose to which their money was being directed. They would like to know that the management team to which they do not belong is acting ethically and in their best interests.

To facilitate this the company, through the auspices of its management, is required to prepare a financial record of the company's financial position and performance at regular intervals and provide copies to the investors. As a minimum this information is provided annually and sanctioned by the investors at an annual general meeting.

However, the concerns of our investor may not be fully relieved as they read of huge frauds perpetrated by management teams in high profile and previously well-respected companies. Classic examples include The Mirror Group, Enron and WorldCom. To minimise these risks investors look to gain additional assurance in the information sent to them, and understandably these safeguards are being continuously improved (Figure 1.2).

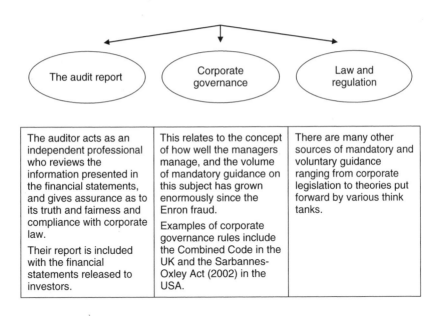

The audit report	Corporate governance	Law and regulation
The auditor acts as an independent professional who reviews the information presented in the financial statements, and gives assurance as to its truth and fairness and compliance with corporate law. Their report is included with the financial statements released to investors.	This relates to the concept of how well the managers manage, and the volume of mandatory guidance on this subject has grown enormously since the Enron fraud. Examples of corporate governance rules include the Combined Code in the UK and the Sarbannes-Oxley Act (2002) in the USA.	There are many other sources of mandatory and voluntary guidance ranging from corporate legislation to theories put forward by various think tanks.

Figure 1.2 Improving investor assurance

These all serve to improve confidence, but never become complacent as rules are designed to be broken, and an auditor can only give reasonable assurance and not a guarantee as it would be unrealistic for them to look at every piece of paper produced by an international corporate giant.

Note that at this stage we will not ask about the underlying purpose for the investment as this will require us to use analytical skills covered later in the text, but typical reasons would include:

1. Capital gain arising from growth in the underlying business
2. A revenue stream in the form of dividends
3. Influence or control over the business by using the votes associated with the shares.

Management accounts vs. financial statements

Let us open this section by establishing an important benchmark, namely the skills you will acquire from this book are equally valid to every variety of financial information you will encounter. It is true that different forms of accounts can be prepared, but the engine room skills that generated them remain the same.

Management accounts are for internal consumption by the management team of the business. Typically they are produced on a monthly basis, and will be discussed at the management and board meetings to appraise the progress of the company. If management are to react quickly to their changing business environment it is vital that there is the minimum delay in the provision of financial information, and hence it is accepted that a broader brush will be applied in their preparation. Key features of this information will include:

1. Greater use of estimates
2. A more varied presentational style designed to highlight commercial issues
3. Inclusion of information that would not be released for external consumption such as variance analysis with budgets and forecasts.

Financial statements could justifiably be called the 'glossies' as for many large companies they are comprehensive documents packed with photographs and charts in addition to the more traditional written and numerical contents, and are released into the public arena. This increased audience, many of whom will be looking at more than one company, puts greater emphasis on comparability, and hence a more formalized structure is needed that can be adopted by all.

In an ideal world every set of financial statements produced across the globe would be produced using the same template – particularly with increased use of the Internet putting information just a key stroke away. As will be described later in this chapter great strides have been taken to realise such harmonization, but there is a long way still to go. It would be expected that within a single country it would be possible to create total comparability but there are still challenges to overcome.

Q: Should a small owner-managed business be required to meet the same rules as a large listed company?

Q: Do financial account proformas prepared for a company also fit perfectly to the needs of a partnership or a sole trader?

Q: Are the reporting needs of a bank or insurance company very different from a high-street retailer, and do these differ from a not-for-profit organization such as a charity?

The stakeholder concept

Historically published financial statements have been prepared primarily for shareholders as the possession of shares and the votes associated with them gives the power to control the operating and financial decisions of the company. These votes are used to appoint or remove directors who head the management team acting on their behalf.

The significance of the investors has not been diminished, but it has also become apparent that there are many other parties who have an interest in the financial position and performance of a company. Grouped together these interested parties represent the stakeholders of the business, and the information that is most relevant to them can be very diverse. A good quality set of financial statements should meet all of these needs – do not forget that you are a stakeholder and as such would want to ensure that adequate information was available to meet your priorities.

Let us consider the needs to different stakeholder groups (Table 1.1).

Visualize a set of financial statements that provides a wide array of quantitative and qualitative information, which provides as much information on corporate and social reporting as it does on the

Table 1.1 Meeting stakeholder needs

Trade creditors	These are the suppliers of the business, and will be keen to evaluate the prospects of default on the money owed to them. Their priorities will be cash and the short-term viability of their customer.
Lenders (e.g. bank)	Cash is important again to meet finance costs and capital repayments, but the longer-term nature of this borrowing implies they will also like to know about the availability of assets to act as security and the longer-term business prospects.
Potential investors	This is heavily influenced by the goals of the individual. If they want a short-term return then cash-rich profits will be desirable from which to pay dividends, but if they are focussed on long-term gain then reinvestment rates and financing will be considered.
Employees	Interests lie in job security, and the prospects for improvements to remuneration.
Government	The Government requires taxable profits for the public coffers, but it is also concerned with qualitative factors such as which sectors of the economy are performing poorly.
Society	This is a more nebulous concept but is gaining more importance as the World strains to sustain consumable resources and the dangers of global warming become apparent. Questions will be asked about the social responsibility of business.

numbers, and that analyses the cash position of the business. Dream no more, as for most companies they already present this information, we just need to know how to find and use it!

Published financial statements are a mine of information if you know where to look!

Jessops plc (2005)

The owner-managed business

For many small companies the division between investors and managers is lost with the same individuals filling both roles. This negates one of the principal reasons for preparing financial statements for an external audience, although management accounts remain a crucial internal control over the operations of the business.

In light of the above it is appropriate that subject to certain constraints small businesses be exempt from the most onerous and expensive requirements of publishing financial statements, but it is equally inappropriate that they be completely exempted given the other stakeholder groups previously identified and the drive towards increased corporate governance.

At the time of publication the criteria designating a small company for accounting purposes in the UK were:

1. Turnover not more than £5.6 million
2. Gross assets not more than £2.8 million
3. Employees not more than 50.

As per the UK rules a company qualifies as small if it meets two of the three criteria and is not a public company, insurance company, company authorised to conduct financial services or a member of an ineligible group of companies (i.e. another member of the group is a public company, etc.).

The potential exemptions given are considerable, and will be revisited in the text as areas of detail are explored.

So much more than numbers

Compare a set of published financial statements from 50 years ago to those of today and the difference would be stark. This is not a reference to any particular point of technical detail, but to the wealth of additional disclosures now included as standard which would not have been seen previously.

To highlight the wealth of information available here is the index (Table 1.2) from the easyJet plc (2005) financial statements with a brief tour guide as what to expect behind the label.

Table 1.2 easyJet (2005) – Financial statement index

Year at a glance	An easy to digest snapshot of some key facts and figures such as changes to revenues and cash flows.
Chairman's statement	A brief 'Big Picture' overview of the business as seen from the top of the management pyramid.
Chief executive's review	More detail than the Chairman's statement with a mix of figures, commentary and diagrams. A great way to get a snapshot of the business and its perceived prospects.
1995–2005 The people and events	As with many large companies the accounts often give additional disclosures beyond those expected that will be of interest to readers or as in this case celebrate a particular highlight (i.e. the tenth anniversary of the company)
Operational and financial review	Although not yet mandatory this is now a common feature of many financial statements. It looks in more detail at issues such as the markets in which the business operates, and its underlying strategy for the long-term financing of the business.
	This can be an invaluable reference when trying to interpret the mainstream financials given later in the report as it gives them business context.
Directors	Brief curriculum vitae of those charged with the running of the company.
Corporate governance	A statement of compliance with corporate governance rules, and brief résumés on key committees such as nominations committee, remuneration committee and audit committee. The latter comprises non-executive directors and acts as a communication channel between the executive board of the company and the external auditors who report on the financial statements.
Social, environmental and ethical report	This represents the largest growth area in corporate reporting – although voluntary companies are increasingly being asked to challenge the concept that short-term profit is always the key objective of management if they are to act in the best interests of the stakeholders. Two of the buzz phrases of modern business are sustainability and social responsibility which cover issues as diverse as the consumption of fossil fuels and minimising pollution to preventing poverty and the use of child labour.
Directors' report	A more formal document, the minimum components of which are set by law.

Table 1.2 easyJet (2005) – Financial statement index—cont'd

Report on directors' remuneration	Another facet of corporate governance as many stakeholders place disproportionate significance upon the remuneration of those charged with running the business. They want to know the basis of remuneration paid, and that incentive schemes are designed to benefit the executive who best promote shareholder value.
Statement of directors' responsibilities	It is important to recognize that the financial statements and their accuracy is the responsibility of the directors and not third parties such as the auditor.
Independent auditor's report	Expressing an opinion on the truth and fairness of the financial statements and their compliance with the law.
Consolidated profit and loss account Consolidated balance sheet Cash flow information Consolidated statement of total recognized gains and losses Consolidated reconciliation of movements in shareholders' funds Notes	These comprise the core elements of traditional financial statements and will be fully examined in the chapters ahead
Company balance sheet Notes to the company balance sheet	The term 'consolidated financial statements' refer to those prepared for a group of companies. However, it is also necessary to give information on the parent company
Summary of selected financial information for 5 years	A mandatory page for listed companies providing a quick reference on trends in key figures.
Shareholder information	Identifies key professionals acting on behalf of the company and significant dates such as that for the annual general meeting.

The things every manager must know

1. Management accounts are focussed on facilitating management decisions whereas financial statements have a more formalized structure that aid comparison of business entities by different stakeholder groups.

2. When conducting analysis of financial information it is important to identify the user as different stakeholder groups have very diverse requirements.

3. Smaller entities are allowed dispensations in the volume and complexity of financial information they have to provide.

4. Financial statements include a wide spectrum of financial and non-financial information on the business with increasing emphasis on issues such as corporate governance and social responsibility.

How are Commercial
Transactions Captured?

The corporate paper trail

Ask any business manager what is important to a business and they will highlight issues such as increasing sales, reducing overheads, promoting the brand and a range of other activities with which most can associate. Many would see it as desirable that they are left alone with the task of growing the business and making it a success, but we must remember that the majority of stakeholders are not a part of these day-to-day activities, and yet remain essential to the business. If the bank will not lend us money or shareholders demand an excess return of their investment this will threaten the entity's existence.

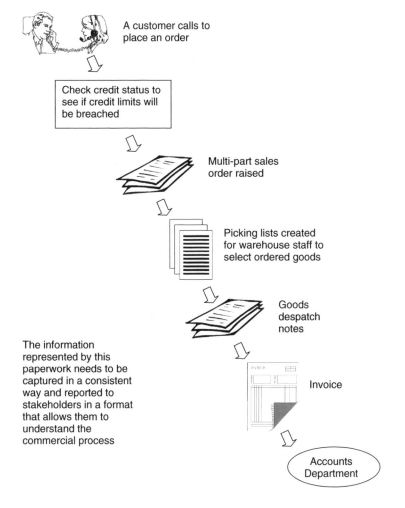

A customer calls to place an order

Check credit status to see if credit limits will be breached

Multi-part sales order raised

Picking lists created for warehouse staff to select ordered goods

Goods despatch notes

The information represented by this paperwork needs to be captured in a consistent way and reported to stakeholders in a format that allows them to understand the commercial process

Invoice

Accounts Department

Figure 2.1 The typical sales process

Consequently the accountant can be seen as a translator converting the day-to-day transactions of a business into a diet that will satisfy these other consumers. Their task is considerable as the volume of transactions completed by many of the multi-national conglomerates of this global age is enormous. As an example think of the steps associated with making a single sale, and match them to those shown in Figure 2.1.

The bank does not want to know about a particular sale, unless it is a make-or-break contract; they want to receive information on the total sales of the entity together with comparative data so that the commercial success of the business and its products can be gauged against previous periods, competitors and so on.

The system used by accountants to capture this information has been in existence for more than 500 years, and is fundamentally the same wherever financial information is prepared in the World.

Capturing the data

To understand the mechanism by which commercial transactions are captured for financial purposes we should consider an example (Example 2.1), but prior to this we need to identify two key principles that will underpin everything we do.

Key principle 1

In a similar way to Newton's third law of physics which states that for every action there is an equal and opposite reaction we can draw an analogy with accounting. If an asset is purchased then the counter to this must be that either cash has been spent or the money is owed to the supplier.

This is the logic that lies behind one of the most important terms in accounting, namely *double entry bookkeeping*.

It is a principle that can never be broken, and will be a vital tool when it comes to analysing financial statements as we must always consider what else will be impacted by the action we take.

Key principle 2

A company is a *separate legal entity* from the shareholders who have invested in it. Hence if money is loaned to the company it is the company which owes the funds back to the lender.

This affirms the logic of the term *limited liability* as the investors in the company cannot be held accountable for its debts. Note that in the case of very small companies that are owner-managed this protection can be illusory as the bank may ask for personal guarantees from the directors/owners as additional security.

Example 2.1

Capturing financial data for a newly established company

On 1st January Mr Big decides to set up a new company, Mr Big Ltd, using the £500,000 he has recently won on the national lottery. He has no accounting knowledge and decides that the best plan is to keep a simple diary of events which can then be handed to his accountant at a later date.

The company is to specialize in the distribution of high quality clothing for those with a love of the outdoors.

The diary for January reads as follows:

Noteworthy event	Description
1	Using the services of a local solicitor the company is incorporated and £500,000 of £1 shares issued.
2	Retail premises were purchased together with some office furniture and a company car. The total cost was £300,000 and this was settled in cash with the various suppliers.
3	A customer list database was also purchased from an existing business for £25,000 cash.
4	The company buys two batches of walking shoes. Both cost £20,000, but supplier A is happy to defer payment such that 50% is received by 28 February and 50% is received on 31 March whilst supplier B demands cash. The individual cost of the boots is £50 per unit from both suppliers.

Continued

Noteworthy event	Description
5	During February Mr Big made sales as follows:
	120 units to Customer X at £90/unit for cash (£10,800)
	250 units to Customer Y at £80/unit for cash (£20,000)
	200 units to Customer Z at £110/unit with payment due in 45 days (£22,000).
6	On 31 January £8,000 is paid to a delivery company for the use of their services for the month.
7	At the end of the month Mr Big realized that his initial cash injection was unlikely to be sufficient to fund a successful set-up period. Consequently prior to the month end he negotiated a £200,000 loan from the bank repayable in 4 years. The loan was received on the last day of the month and hence no interest will fall due until February.

Remember for every action taken by the management team (currently just Mr Big) there has to be an equal reaction. Let us identify the two elements for each of the transactions of Mr Big Ltd.

Noteworthy Event	Action		Reaction	
1	Using the services of a local solicitor the company is incorporated and £500,000 of £1 shares issued.			
	Cash	Increases	Share Capital	Increases
2	Retail premises were purchased together with some office furniture and a company car. The total cost was £300,000 and this was settled in cash with the various suppliers.			
	Premises, etc.	Increase	Cash	Decreases
3	A customer list database was also purchased from an existing business for £25,000 cash.			
	Customer list	Increases	Cash	Decreases
4	The company buys two batches of walking shoes. Both cost £20,000, but supplier A is happy to defer payment such that 50% is received by 28 February and 50% is received on 31 March whilst supplier B demands cash. The individual cost of the boots is £50 per unit from each supplier.			
	Walking shoes (i.e. stock)	Increase	Cash (£20,000)	Decrease
			Creditors (£20,000)	Increase

Noteworthy Event	Action			Reaction	
5	During February Mr Big made sales as follows:				
	120 units to Customer X at £90/unit for cash (£10,800)				
	250 units to Customer Y at £80/unit for cash (£20,000)				
	200 units to Customer Z at £110/unit with payment due in 45 days (£22,000)				
	Cash (£30,800)	Increases		Stock (570 units at £50 each = £28,500)	Decreases
	Debtors (£22,000)	Increase		Profit (Balance = £24,300)	Increases
6	On 31 January £8000 is paid to a delivery company for the use of their services for the month.				
	Profit	Decreases	Cash		Decreases
7	At the end of the month Mr Big realized that his initial cash injection was unlikely to be sufficient to fund a successful set-up period. Consequently prior to the month end he negotiated a £200,000 loan from the bank repayable in 4 years. The loan was received on the last day of the month and hence no interest will fall due until February.				
	Cash	Increases	Loan		Increases

As you review the double entry in the table above you may be asking if it matters which entry is put on the left and which on the right. At the moment it makes no difference to the underlying logic, but when we later examine accounting conventions this would be very significant to an accountant.

It should be noted that although the accounting world is constantly striving to move towards global uniformity there are currently several items which are given different labels depending upon where the data originated. This is particularly true of the following:

Table 2.1 Comparable terminology	
UK Terminology [as used above]	International Terminology
Stock	Inventory
Debtors	Receivables
Creditors	Payables

The accounting equation

If you are Mr Big, the owner of the shares issued in Example 2.1, then you would want to track your investment, and would want to see how your money is being put to work. For the small number of transactions undertaken since incorporation you would obtain a full record of activity simply by reading the diary already prepared, but if we had invested in a huge conglomerate with millions of transactions over a stipulated period this would be totally inappropriate. Clearly we need a system that allows a compromise between the two.

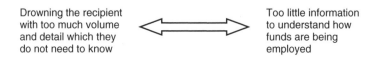

Drowning the recipient with too much volume and detail which they do not need to know ⟷ Too little information to understand how funds are being employed

To facilitate comparison a common basis has been developed for disclosing the performance and position of a business. This is based around the accounting equation:

$$\text{Fixed assets} + \text{Current assets} - \text{Current liabilities} - \text{Non-current liabilities} = \text{Share capital} + \text{Reserves}$$

Let us consider the typical features of the main components of the equation:

Fixed assets (also known as non-current assets)

◆ Held for long-term use (i.e. more than 1 year) in the business
◆ Not traded as part of the business's core activities
◆ They can be tangible or intangible

Per Mr Big Limited

The premises, furniture and company all represent tangible fixed assets of the business. They will be bought and sold at irregular intervals to meet operational needs, but are not actively traded on a day-to-day basis.

> *Tangible fixed assets = £300,000*
>
> The customer list is also a fixed asset, but is considered an intangible asset as it has no physical form.
>
> *Intangible fixed assets = £25,000*

Current assets

- ◆ Typically will be used within 1 year although for certain types of industry this may be a longer period due to the protracted nature of their operating cycle (i.e. the period between the date when a sale is initiated and the final receipt of the proceeds)
- ◆ Directly linked to the operating activities of the business.

> Per Mr Big Limited
>
> The stock, debtors and cash balances all represent current assets of the business.
>
> The walking shoes represent stock as these are the items held exclusively for sale, and not for long-term use within the business.
>
> $Stock = [(2 \times £20,000) - (570 \times £50)] = £11,500$
>
> $Debtors = £22,000$
>
> *Cash*
>
> | | Cash IN (£) | Cash OUT (£) |
> |---|---|---|
> | Share issue | 500,000 | |
> | Tangible fixed assets | | 300,000 |
> | Intangible fixed assets | | 25,000 |
> | Stock | | 20,000 |
> | Sale of stock | 30,800 | |
> | Payment for deliveries | | 8,000 |
> | Loan | 200,000 | |
> | | 730,800 | 353,000 |
> | | (353,000) | |
> | Net cash position | 377,800 | |
>
> *Total current assets = £411,300*

Current liabilities

♦ As for current assets

> Per Mr Big Limited
>
> The creditors will represent a current liability as the suppliers of the walking shoes will not be prepared to wait in excess of a year without receiving the cash for the goods they have allowed the company to receive on credit terms.
>
> *Creditors = £20,000*

Long-term liabilities

♦ Usually long-term funding repayable in more than 1 year

> Per Mr Big Limited
>
> The loan from the bank is repayable in 4 years and hence would fall into this category.
>
> *Long-term liabilities = £200,000*

Share capital

♦ When a company incorporates it issues a number of ordinary shares to the founders of the business
♦ There is no stipulated number, and hence this will vary from company to company
♦ Each share has a face value known as its par value
♦ Post-incorporation as the company grows the true worth of each share will differ from its par value, and this is most clearly seen for those shares of companies listed on a stock exchange where the value of the shares varies from minute to minute depending on the demand from investors.

> Per Mr Big Limited
>
> The company has issued 500,000 shares each with a par value of £1
>
> *Share capital = £500,000*

Reserves

As a company trades it will make a profit or loss on the trading transactions it completes. Ultimately this profit or loss is attributed to the investors in the business, but this will become more apparent if we now complete the accounting equation for Mr Big Limited.

Example 2.2

Applying the accounting equation

Fixed Assests	Current Assests	Current Liabilities	Long-Term Liabilities	Share Capital	Reserves

£325,000 + £411,300 − £20,000   − £20,000   = £500,000 + ?

Hence:

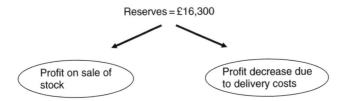

Reserves = £16,300

Profit on sale of stock

Profit decrease due to delivery costs

Taken together the share capital and reserves of the company are referred to as the *equity* but as we develop our understanding of accounting never lose sight of what lies behind this headline term.

The key feature of the accounting equation is that it must always balance. This is intuitively true as equal and opposite entries were recorded for every transaction and hence however the equation is presented the two sides will always be equal (Figure 2.2).

ASSETS £736,300	−	LIABILITIES £220,000	=	EQUITY £516,300
ASSETS £736,300	=	EQUITY £516,300	+	LIABILITIES £220,000

Figure 2.2 Alternative presentation of the accounting equation

The things every manager must know

1. The dual entry principle underpins the mechanism by which commercial data is captured and translated into accounting entries. Every transaction creates two effects that are always equal in size.

2. Companies represent separate legal entities that conduct transactions in their own name through the medium of the management team assigned to run them. The members of the management team may change but the company remains constant.

3. The accounting equation:

The Balance Sheet: A Freeze Frame & The Concept of Articulation Using the Profit and Loss Account

Linking the separate legal entity concept to the balance sheet

The separate legal entity concept underpins the accounting equation as the latter summarizes what the business owns and owes, but most investors would not be impressed if the total record they received from their investment was

This would not enable them to answer key questions essential to help their understanding.

Q: What proportion of the liabilities are associated with long-term funding?

Q: Is my money being invested in fixed assets with the aim of generating capital growth or has it been directed to the purchase of stock to facilitate increased sales?

The solution is a document that contains more information in a consistent format, but which rarely exceeds one side in length. The document produced is known as a balance sheet and represents a freeze frame of what the business owns and owes at a particular moment in time.

In the UK the classic format of the balance sheet is as shown in Illustration 3.1, and it can be seen that it mirrors the three classic sections of the accounting equation.

1. Assets
2. Liabilities
3. Equity

The data collected for Mr Big Ltd (Chapter 2) can now be represented in this format (Example 3.1.)

		£	£
Fixed assets			
Intangible assets			X
Tangible assets			
Land and buildings		X	
Plant and machinery		X	
Fixtures, fittings, tools and equipment		X̲	X
Investments			X̲
			X
Current assets			
Stocks		X	
Debtors		X	
Investments		X	
Cash at bank and in hand		X̲	
		X	

① (bracket grouping Fixed assets, Investments and Current assets)

		£	£
Creditors: amounts falling due within 1 year			
Trade creditors		X	
Net current assets (liabilities)			X
Total assets less current liabilities			
Creditors: amounts falling due after more than 1 year			
Bank loans and overdrafts			X̲
			X̲

② (bracket grouping Creditors and Net current assets section)

		£	£
Capital and reserves			
Share capital			X
Reserves			X̲
			X̲

③ (bracket grouping Capital and reserves)

Illustration 3.1 UK balance sheet format

Example 3.1

Balance sheet of Mr Big Ltd as at 31 January

	£	£
Fixed assets		
Intangible assets		25,000
Tangible assets		300,000
		325,000
Current assets		
Stocks	11,500	
Debtors	22,000	
Cash at bank and in hand	377,800	
	411,300	
Creditors: amounts falling due within 1 year		
Trade creditors	20,000	
Net current assets		391,300
Total assets less current liabilities		
Creditors: amounts falling due after more than 1 year		
Bank loans		(200,000)
		516,300
Capital and reserves		
Share capital		500,000
Reserves		16,300
		516,300

NOTE: All the figures on the balance sheet can be directly validated with the exception of the reserves.

◆ Stock and fixed assets can be physically viewed
◆ Debtors and the bank could be asked to confirm outstanding balances, etc.

Given that every transaction has two equal sides the reserves can confidently be completed as the balancing figure, but to conduct meaningful analysis this figure must be explored more fully.

The purpose of the balance sheet

As we build our understanding of financial statements and their analysis it will become apparent that the balance sheet is the lynch-pin of modern accounting. We have already noted that it is a reflection of the accounting equation, but adds some flesh to the bones by providing a sub-analysis of the component parts. Each of these sub-categories will be explored in detail as we progress, but there is no time like the present to familiarize ourselves with the basics!

Fixed assets: These assets can be divided into three distinct types:

1. *Tangible*: These have physical substance such as plant and machinery.
2. *Intangible*: Lack physical substance but often have considerable value such as brands.
3. *Investments*: When a business invests in the shares of another company with a view to the long-term rather than short-term trading.

Current Assets: These form part of the working capital of the business, namely assets used in the day-to-day operations. Did you notice anything about the format of the current assets in the balance sheet? You should have observed that they are in the order of increasing liquidity.

1. *Stock*: Has yet to be sold and hence is the least liquid.
2. *Debtors*: Represent money collectable on credit sales already made.
3. *Cash*: For analysis purposes the levels of cash in the business will be key to our understanding of its viability.

The investments held within current assets are those held for trading or with the intention to dispose within the next year.

Creditors falling due within 1 year: This broad title shields one of the most diverse sections of the balance sheet as it includes the negative component of working capital in the form of trade creditors (i.e. amounts owed to suppliers) and overdrafts plus amounts owing for tax, interest and dividends.

Creditors falling due after 1 year: Includes long-term debt finance of the business.

Share capital: Remember this is the par value of the shares.

Some companies will have more than one class of share capital (e.g. ordinary and preference), and deciding upon the classification of these different classes will be vital in our analysis of the financial information.

Reserves: Together with the share capital these represent the theoretical amount that would be owed to the owners of the business if it were to be wound up, but to understand this more fully we need to look beyond the balance sheet.

The purpose of the profit and loss account (also referred to as the income statement)

A company will produce a balance sheet at the close of the financial year for inclusion in the published accounts, and monthly for inclusion in the management accounts that are presented to the board of directors to facilitate decisions about the future direction of the business. We know that the balance sheet represents a freeze frame in time, but surely the directors need more information about the activities of the business that link these freeze frames, and this is the purpose of the profit and loss account (also referred to as the income statement).

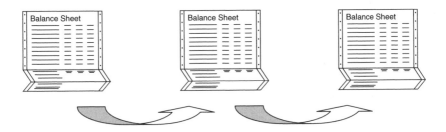

As with the balance sheet the format of the profit and loss account has a standardized layout to facilitate inter-company comparison, but the basic concept is one with which we are all familiar – goods are sold but this incurs costs and the balance between earnings and expenses will dictate if we make a profit or a loss. The standardized format is shown in Illustration 3.2, but we can already prepare a profit and loss statement for Mr Big Ltd (Example 3.2).

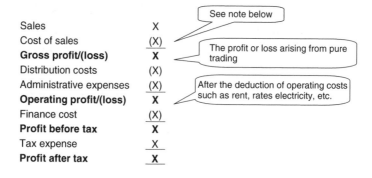

Sales	X
Cost of sales	(X)
Gross profit/(loss)	**X**
Distribution costs	(X)
Administrative expenses	(X)
Operating profit/(loss)	**X**
Finance cost	(X)
Profit before tax	**X**
Tax expense	X
Profit after tax	**X**

See note below

The profit or loss arising from pure trading

After the deduction of operating costs such as rent, rates electricity, etc.

Illustration 3.2 Profit and loss account for the period ending...

Example 3.2

Profit and loss account of Mr Big Ltd for the month ended 31 January...

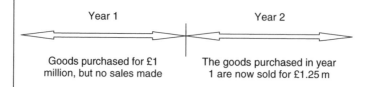

	£
Sales	52,800
Cost of sales	(28,500)
Trading profit/(loss)	**24,300**
Distribution expenses	(8,000)
Operating profit/(loss)	**16,300**

570 pairs of shoes were sold each having a unit cost of £50

Note: The cost of sales brings us into contact with our third key principle of accounting.

Key principle 3

To understand the *Concept of Matching* consider the following:

Year 1	Year 2
Goods purchased for £1 million, but no sales made	The goods purchased in year 1 are now sold for £1.25 m

Intuitively we all know a profit of £250,000 has been made on the purchase and subsequent sale of the goods, but unless we apply the concept of matching this is not what a user of the financial statements will see. Instead when the financial statements for year 1 are delivered the user will be horrified to see a £1m loss, and then 12 months later will believe there has been a phenomenal turnaround when the year 2 financial statements show a profit of £1.25 m.

The reality is that in year 1 there has been a simple exchange of assets – cash in exchange for a stock of goods to sell in the future. Consequently the £1m should not be recognised as a cost in year 1 but carried forward and matched against the revenue derived from their sale in year 2.

This is what happens in a set of accounts but is cunningly hidden behind the label 'Cost of sales'.

			£
		Opening stock	X
Cost of Sales	=	*Add* Purchases in period	X
			X
		Less Closing stock	(X)
			X

In the case of Mr Big Ltd the data collected related to the first month of trading and hence the opening stock was zero.

			£
		Opening stock	Nil
Mr Big Ltd	=	Purchases in period	40,000
Cost of Sales			40,000
		Less Closing stock	(11,500)
			28,500

The closing stock comprises of 230 pairs of shoes with a unit price of £50.

The point of articulation

The profit and loss account can be viewed as a transient document which records the activity of a period and then disappears, but in so doing it serves two vital functions:

1. It provides a user with a rich source of data to which key analytical tools can be applied to ascertain a better understanding of the business. Typical examples would be the gross and net profit margins.
2. The profit or loss calculated acts as the link between successive balance sheets and consequently this number has become known as the point of articulation. This is demonstrated in Figure 3.1.

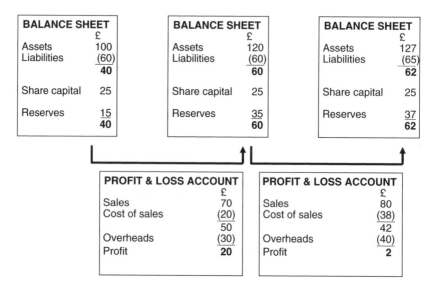

Figure 3.1 The point of articulation

At the end of each period the profit and loss account has served its purpose, namely capturing the activities of the period, and then is effectively collapsed down to its definitive component, namely the profit or loss for the period. This result is added or subtracted from the reserves of the company in the balance sheet, and hence links consecutive balance sheets together. However, it is not enough to simply understand the mathematics; if we are to understand the story being told by the financial statements we need to know the logic for the transfer.

When we encountered the accounting equation it was established that the equity of a company was equal to its assets less any outstanding liabilities, but this can be viewed in a subtlety different way. Let us return to the story of Mr Big and the company he has established.

Scenario 1

To establish the company Mr Big injected £500,000 of his own money into the company, and in return received shares of an equivalent value.

Imagine he had a sudden change of heart, and immediately closed the company what would he expect to receive?

Yes: £500,000 – his original investment (in reality minus some substantial administration fees). Hence the shares represent a type of liability to the business, but the key difference is that the amounts outstanding are not due to third parties such as the suppliers of the company but to the owner.

Scenario 2

Mr Big Ltd successfully trades and makes a profit of £16,300 over its first month of operations before a decision was made by Mr Big to close the company and invest his funds into a separate project. How much will Mr Big now expect to receive from the closure, assuming that costs of discontinuance are ignored?

The answer is £516,300, as the profit generated by the business is ultimately attributable to the owner(s), and when the company is wound up they will expect repayment.

It is vital that as an aspiring analyst of financial statements you understand the principles discussed above, but I am sure that you are also starting to consider the practicalities and asking questions such as:

◆ Is it likely that assets sold will realise exactly their stated value in the balance sheet?
◆ If a company has built up a good reputation a prospective purchaser will be asked to pay for this intangible asset, and yet it will not be on the balance sheet as it will never have been purchased

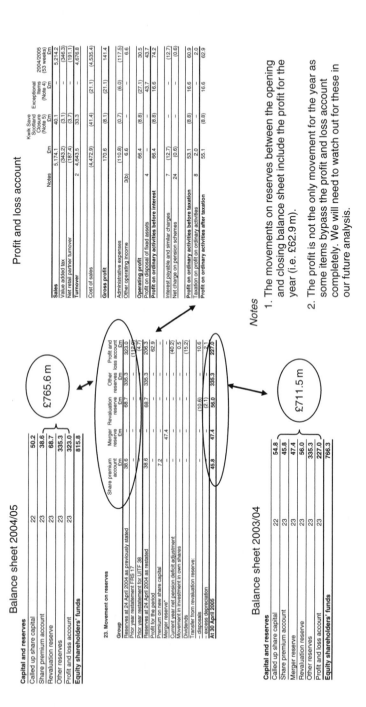

Figure 3.2 Financial statement articulation – Somerfield plc (2004/05)

previously. Can such items ever be reflected in the balance sheet, and if not surely this undermines the 'value' of the financial statements as a tool for understanding the business?

The truth is that financial statements do have limitations which will be explored more fully as we build our knowledge, but if these are known and understood by the user there is a wealth of information just waiting to be released.

The real world

Figure 3.2 shows the articulation of the financial statements of a large supermarket chain. It must be remembered that unlike Mr Big Ltd which has traded for a single period Somerfield plc has traded for many years, and at the close of each period its profit has been accumulated within the reserves. Hence it is not possible to reconcile the opening and closing positions for a given year without reference to the supporting notes which give a sub-analysis of the figures.

It is also important to realise that the owners of a business are unlikely to wait until the cessation of trade before they recoup a return on their investment. Each year they will draw some of their entitlement in the form of dividends, and the reserves of the business will be reduced accordingly. Consideration will need to be given to the amount drawn from the business as too severe a depletion of cash may impair growth potential, and ultimately serve to the long-term detriment of the owner through reduced profits.

The things every manager must know

1. Equity represents the owner's interest in the business, and theoretically would be the amount owed thereto if the business was to be terminated.
2. The profit earned for the period acts as a point of articulation between the opening and closing balance sheets.
3. The matching principle dictates that costs should be recognized in the same period as the revenues they helped to generate.

A Brief Look at the
Accountants' Phrase Book

Understanding the label

Imagine you have been transported from a 1950s tea room to the modern equivalent – as you approach the counter a friendly assistant asks would you like a grande skinny mocha! My guess is that you would look bemused, but if they had described the same beverage as a large coffee with a hint of chocolate you would have gratefully accepted their offer.

A similar situation exists with accountants who many believe speak in a coded language, but like many codes the true meaning appears obvious once deciphered. The great news is that based on the earlier chapters you already understand the basic dynamics that underpin a set of financial statements; we simply need to add the labels used by accountants for the same things.

Follow the paper trail described in Figure 4.1, and you will see several terms that you will have encountered when presented with financial information in the past, but you will now be able to visualise these in practical terms.

We have just one bridge left to cross and then we can speak freely in the accountants' language. All transactions have two equal components, but if the trial balance referred to in the illustration is to be prepared we need to ensure consistency as to which items are recorded in which list or else there is a recipe for chaos. We need to tackle the concept of debits and credits.

Debits and credits

Unless you happen to be an expert chemist or physicist, when asked questions such as 'why is the sky blue?' we are likely to reply 'because it is', and this is an excellent start point for tackling the subject of debits and credits. Do not waste valuable time looking for the inner meaning to these terms because we could equally be using the labels chalk and cheese!

As an analyst of financial information you simply need to be aware of the rules that apply to these labels so that you can add value in a report or meeting when the financial guru starts to throw these terms into the conversation.

Diary Entry = Journal Entry

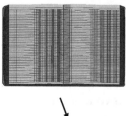

Each transaction was initially recorded in a diary so that the information would not be lost, with each diary entry comprising of two equal effects (e.g. a £1000 cash acquisition of a car would result in a diary entry which reduced cash and increased fixed assets by this amount). An accountant would describe each double-sided diary entry as *a journal.*

Ledger

At regular intervals the journals are posted to a *ledger*, traditionally a book but in modern times usually held in electronic form.
Each page of the ledger is known as an account, and is used to capture all the entries to a similar category (i.e. all cash items, all fixed assets).

Trial Balance

	£	£
Bank	X	
Cash	X	
Stock	X	
Sales		X
	X	**X**

Prior to the preparation of the monthly management accounts or the year end 'glossy' accounts a *trial balance* is completed. This takes the total from each account in the ledger and presents it in list form. Two lists are prepared and if the two lists are not equal then the accountant knows an error has been made.

'Glossy' Financial Statements = The Finished Product

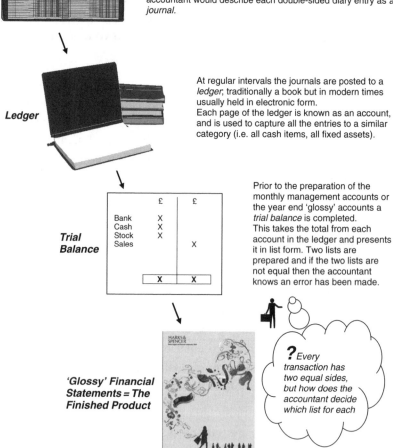

? Every transaction has two equal sides, but how does the accountant decide which list for each

Figure 4.1 Understanding the accountants' code

Here are the rules:

BALANCE SHEET

	DEBIT	CREDIT
	Asset increases	Asset decreases
	Liability decreases	Liability increases

PROFIT AND LOSS

	DEBIT	CREDIT
	Income decreases	Income increases
	Expenses increase	Expenses decrease

Every transaction will result in a journal with an equal number of debits and credits.

For example, When Mr Big Ltd purchased furniture and equipment for £300,000 an accountant would record this as follows:

Debit   Fixed assets   £300,000
Credit   Cash   £300,000

Note that by convention accountants place debits on the left and credits on the right.

It is also now clear how the two lists comprising the trial balance are generated – one is the listing of all debit totals and the other a list of all credit totals. Intuitively they must be equal, but in the real world problems can arise.

1. In a manual system it is common for errors to be made when dealing with large volumes of transactions – numbers can be transposed or even missed entirely. The total of debits and credits will now differ, and it is common practice to create a quick fix by inserting a balancing figure in the form of a *suspense account*. If the systems of the business are good and there is strong corporate governance the problems that created the necessity for the suspense account must be tackled quickly and the correcting journals posted to ensure accuracy in the figures presented to the board or shareholders.
2. Many computerized accounting systems will not accept a journal where the debits and credits do not balance, but this does not prevent the correct amount being posted to the wrong account in the ledger.

Confusion arising from day-to-day usage

'Debits' and 'credits' are terms that most of us encounter on a regular basis when we receive a statement from the bank, but this is often a cause of confusion. If the bank tells you that your account is in credit we view this as good news implying that we have money in our account, and yet our financial use of the term appears to be in direct conflict with this interpretation. To an accountant a credit balance implies a liability rather than an asset (Figure 4.2).

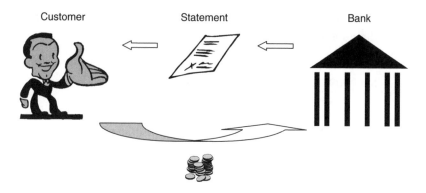

Figure 4.2 A different perspective of debits and credits

> When the customer places money into his account he has the right
> to withdraw this at any time as he is the legal owner. Hence from
> the bank's perspective this money is a liability as it is effectively
> owed back to the customer.
>
> On the statement received the bank will say the account is in
> credit as the paperwork is prepared from their viewpoint and not
> that of the customer.

Mr Big Ltd revisted

Set out below are the original journals for Mr Big Ltd's first month of
operations, but this time it is shown using the language of accountants; take a moment to check that you have understood the rules.

Journals	Debit		Credit	
1	Using the services of a local solicitor the company is incorporated and £500,000 of £1 shares issued.			
	Cash Account	Debit	Share Capital Account	Credit
2	Retail premises were purchased together with some office furniture and a company car. The total cost was £300,000 and this was settled in cash with the various suppliers.			
	Fixed Asset Account	Debit	Cash Account	Credit

Journals	Debit		Credit	
3	A customer list database was also purchased from an existing business for £25,000 cash.			
	Intangible Asset Account	Debit	Cash Account	Credit
4	The company buys two batches of walking shoes. Both cost £20,000, but supplier A is happy to defer payment such that 50% is received by 28 February and 50% is received on 31 March whilst supplier B demands cash. The individual cost of the boots is £50 per unit from both suppliers.			
	Purchases Account	Debit	Cash Account (£20,000)	Credit
			Creditors Account (£20,000)	Credit
5	During February Mr Big made sales as follows: 120 units to Customer X at £90/unit for cash (£10,800) 250 units to Customer Y at £80/unit for cash (£20,000) 200 units to Customer Z at £110/unit with payment due in 45 days (£22,000).			
	Cash Account (£30,800)	Debit	Sales (£52,800)	Credit
	Debtors Account (£22,000)	Debit		
6	On 31 January £8,000 is paid to a delivery company for the use of their services for the month.			
	Distribution Expense Account	Debit	Cash Account	Credit
7	At the end of the month Mr Big realized that his initial cash injection was unlikely to be sufficient to fund a successful set-up period. Consequently prior to the month end he negotiated a £200,000 loan from the bank repayable in 4 years. The loan was received on the last day of the month and hence no interest will fall due until February.			
	Cash Account	Debit	Loan Account	Credit

This terminology can then be superimposed on the financial statements themselves.

Example 4.1

– Profit and loss account of Mr Big Ltd for the month ending 31 January...

	£	
Sales	52,800	Credit
Cost of sales	(28,500)	Debit
Trading profit/(loss)	**24,300**	
Distribution expenses	(8,000)	Debit
Operating profit/(loss)	**16,300**	

> Note that a net profit equates to an overall surplus of credits. Hence the point of articulation concept still holds as the reserves at the foot of the balance sheet are also credit figures (in this case), and the profit will be added on to this balance (i.e. credit + credit).

Example 4.2

Balance sheet of Mr Big Ltd as at 31 January . . .

	£	£	
Fixed assets			
Intangible assets		25,000	Debit
Tangible assets		300,000	Debit
		325,000	
Current assets			
Stocks	11,500		Debit
Debtors	22,000		Debit
Cash at bank and in hand	377,800		Debit
	411,300		
Creditors: amounts falling due within 1 year			
Trade creditors	20,000		Credit
Net current assets		391,300	
Total assets less current liabilities			
Creditors: amounts falling due after more than 1 year			
Bank loans		(200,000)	Credit
		516,300	
Capital and reserves			
Share capital		500,000	Credit
Reserves		16,300	Credit
		516,300	

The things every manager must know

1. Accounting terminology is no more than some unique labels being applied to core concepts that are easy to grasp.
   a. Journal – A two-sided diary entry used to initially record a transaction.

b. Account – A collection pot for items of a similar nature (e.g. all stock or cash).

c. Ledger – A collection of accounts.

d. Trial Balance – A listing of the outstanding balance on each account in the ledger at a point in time.

e. Suspense Account – A temporary account used to balance a trial balance whilst the error(s) that have caused an imbalance are located.

2. Do not worry about the terms 'debit' and 'credit' in your own day-to-day analysis, but be aware of the basic rules that support these terms in case they are included in external material that you need to incorporate within your own work.

Cash and Corporate
Survival

Making profit does not mean you can pay the bills

Consider the following sequence of events and see if you can match the story to situations you have seen or read about in the press.

Scenario: Rapid Growth plc is a listed company specializing in the manufacture and sale of household furniture. The company has built a reputation for high quality products, and over recent years has achieved an annual growth rate of 12 per cent per annum; it is seen as one of the rising stars in the sector and its share price is buoyant.

In line with good corporate governance recommendations the senior management team have a remuneration package that is linked to corporate performance in the form of profit-related pay and share options. The directors had grown concerned because in spite of the company's continued success their revenue and profit projections showed a slowing in growth to 7 per cent. Although commendable they knew that market analysts might perceive this negatively and the consequence would be a fall in the share price which they wanted to avoid.

Let us consider their potential time line to disaster.

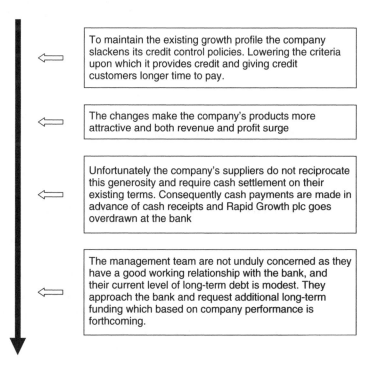

To maintain the existing growth profile the company slackens its credit control policies. Lowering the criteria upon which it provides credit and giving credit customers longer time to pay.

The changes make the company's products more attractive and both revenue and profit surge

Unfortunately the company's suppliers do not reciprocate this generosity and require cash settlement on their existing terms. Consequently cash payments are made in advance of cash receipts and Rapid Growth plc goes overdrawn at the bank

The management team are not unduly concerned as they have a good working relationship with the bank, and their current level of long-term debt is modest. They approach the bank and request additional long-term funding which based on company performance is forthcoming.

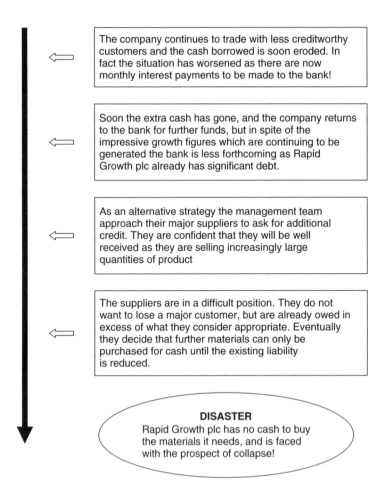

The company continues to trade with less creditworthy customers and the cash borrowed is soon eroded. In fact the situation has worsened as there are now monthly interest payments to be made to the bank!

Soon the extra cash has gone, and the company returns to the bank for further funds, but in spite of the impressive growth figures which are continuing to be generated the bank is less forthcoming as Rapid Growth plc already has significant debt.

As an alternative strategy the management team approach their major suppliers to ask for additional credit. They are confident that they will be well received as they are selling increasingly large quantities of product

The suppliers are in a difficult position. They do not want to lose a major customer, but are already owed in excess of what they consider appropriate. Eventually they decide that further materials can only be purchased for cash until the existing liability is reduced.

DISASTER
Rapid Growth plc has no cash to buy the materials it needs, and is faced with the prospect of collapse!

The situation described above is known as *overtrading*, and demonstrates that cash and profit are two very different concepts. Profit is desirable, but cash usually determines short-term survival – the ideal is to generate cash-rich profits.

Cash accounting vs. accruals accounting

Cash accounting is most commonly seen in small not-for-profit organisations such as a local sports club. The treasurer is unlikely to be a qualified accountant and will simply keep a running tab of cash received from members when they arrive for training and cash outgoings such as payments to the local council for use of the facilities. The concept of cash accounting is also retained within some specialist business sectors such as legal firms, but for the majority of larger entities it would not result in the financial statements giving a true and fair view.

We have already encountered the fundamentals of accruals accounting when looking at the calculation of the cost of sales – Unused stock was deducted from costs and effectively carried forward to future periods where it could be matched against the revenues generated from its sale. However, the best illustration comes from consideration of accruals and prepayments.

Accruals and prepayments

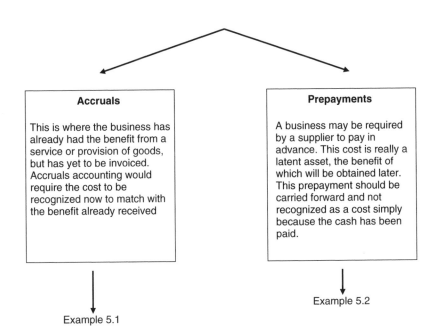

Accruals

This is where the business has already had the benefit from a service or provision of goods, but has yet to be invoiced. Accruals accounting would require the cost to be recognized now to match with the benefit already received

Example 5.1

Prepayments

A business may be required by a supplier to pay in advance. This cost is really a latent asset, the benefit of which will be obtained later. This prepayment should be carried forward and not recognized as a cost simply because the cash has been paid.

Example 5.2

Example 5.1

Accruing for telephone usage costs

Unless you have agreed a flat rate charge a mobile telephone company cannot invoice you in advance as they have no idea of what usage you will incur over the chargeable period.

XYZ plc has a 31 December year end and is invoiced monthly for all the mobile telephones used by its many sales staff. The following information is available to the finance manager who is preparing draft figures for the year-end financial statements.

	Value of invoice received for usage in previous month	Cash paid to telephone company
	£'000	£'000
January	500	535
February	550	500
March	480	550
April	690	480
May	710	690
June	660	710
July	590	660
August	410	590
September	390	410
October	630	390
November	680	630
December	520	680

The company has a policy of paying amounts outstanding at the end of the month following the month in which the invoice was physically received.

Advocates of cash accounting would find it easy to prepare their profit and loss account, as the telephone cost for each month would simply be the cash payment made in that period.

For example, November telephone expense = £630,000

But this is very misleading as the £630,000 is settlement of an invoice received in October for telephone usage in September!

The real cost of telephones used in November is only £520,000, meaning that the November management accounts presented to the board of directors has overstated costs and understated profit by £110,000.

If this disparity is rolled forward to the year end and the preparation of the financial statements that will be made available to shareholders, consider the consequences. The cash accountant will record a December cost of £680,000, but those using accruals accounting face a dilemma as the invoice for December usage will not be received until after the year end date. It will be necessary to make an estimate based on factors such as:

◆ Prior year comparative adjusted for supplier price changes
◆ Changes to the number of sales staff
◆ Idiosyncrasies unique to the business, such as a large sales drive just prior to the year end.

If the estimate is £510,000 this needs to be incorporated within the accounts using the rules of two-sided entry (double-entry bookkeeping as it is often known).

Increase an expense (telephone costs)	£510,000
Increase an accrual (no cash has been paid yet)	£510,000

The accrual will be included as a liability falling due within 1 year on the balance sheet – presumably to be paid in February of the following year in accordance with the company's existing policy.

This is a great time to reaffirm you understood the point of articulation concept covered earlier.

If expenses are increased by £510,000 then profits will fall by a corresponding amount. This means that the amount transferred to reserves in the balance sheet at the end of the period will also be lower by £510,000, but the balance sheet will still balance as liabilities have also been increased by the corresponding accrual leading to reduced net assets.

Example 5.2

Paying for an expense in advance

On 1 January XYZ Ltd insured its head office building for the year ahead at a cost of £3,000 settling with the insurance company via a cheque payment. What impact will this transaction have on the management accounts prepared at the end of January?

Cash Accounting: recognizes the full £3,000 as an expense as the cash has been paid.

Accruals Accounting: The reduction in cash of £3,000 cannot be ignored but on a prorata basis the true expense for January is only £250 with the remaining balance representing a £2,750 prepayment for the 11 months ahead. The prepayment would be recognised as a current asset in the balance sheet as it will be used within 1 year.

It is only accruals accounting that actually matches the cost of the insurance with the period over which benefit is gained from the cover, and it is this method that will be used in the preparation of the accounts.

Satisfying the needs of stakeholders who want to know about both profit and cash

A company has many stakeholders (management, government, shareholders, etc) and it is important to their understanding of a business that they are provided with more information on performance than simply what profit or loss it made for the period.

Let us return to Mr Big Ltd to illustrate these concerns. The company made a profit of £16,300 during its first period of trading, but how does this compare to its cash position, and has this worsened or improved over the equivalent period? Reference to the balance sheet tells us that the closing cash position is £377,800, but if a true appreciation is to be obtained about the financial health of the business we need answers to some further questions.

- ◆ What is the rate of cash burn and is it likely to erode cash balances such that additional long-term funding will be needed from the providers of finance?
- ◆ Are the operations of the business generating net cash inflows or outflows?

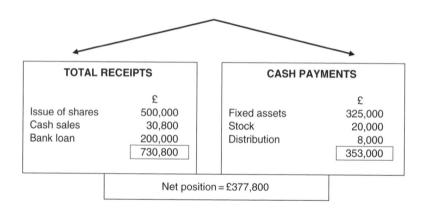

TOTAL RECEIPTS		CASH PAYMENTS	
	£		£
Issue of shares	500,000	Fixed assets	325,000
Cash sales	30,800	Stock	20,000
Bank loan	200,000	Distribution	8,000
	730,800		353,000

Net position = £377,800

♦ Have one-off cash flows distorted the true cash position of the business?

Immediate observations:

♦ Cash receipts have been bolstered by two large one-off items unassociated with trading.
♦ Similarly cash payments are inflated by the purchase of capital assets for long-term use in the business.
♦ Operating cash flows show a net inflow of £2,800. This is very impressive as the company has just completed its first month of trading and cash receipts would be expected to be low.
♦ The operating cash flows are substantially lower than the operating profit as would be expected for a start-up, but if this continued in the long-term it would place stress upon the liquidity of the business.

Formalizing cash flow presentation

In the UK a typical cash flow presentation would be as shown in Illustration 5.1, and this would be given equal prominence in the published financial statements to the balance sheet and the profit and loss account.

	£'000	£'000
Net cash inflow from operating activities (note 1)		5,000
Returns on investment and servicing of finance		
Interest received	1,123	
Interest paid	(68)	
		1,055
Taxation		(2,222)
Capital expenditure		
Payments to acquire tangible fixed assets	(1,356)	
Receipts from sale of tangible fixed assets	251	
		(1,105)
Equity dividends paid		(1,500)
Management of liquid resources		
Purchase of treasury bills	(420)	
Sale of treasury bills	120	
		(300)
Financing		
Issue of ordinary share capital	1,100	
Repurchase of debenture loan	(858)	
Expenses paid in connection with share issues	(12)	
		230
Increase in cash		948

Illustration 5.1 Cash flow statement proforma

Initial skills needed to interpret the cash flow statement.

1. *Think cash*

   A cash flow statement shows exactly what its name implies and so do not be tempted to include accruals or other non-cash movements, but remember that overdrafts are viewed as part of the cash position (simply negative cash).

2. *Calculating cash movements for the period*

   Although we will encounter some embellishments as we build our skill set the basic calculation of numbers to be included in the cash flow statement is:

	£
Opening balance sheet balance	X
Profit and loss account movement	X
Closing balance sheet balance	(X)
Cash movement	**X/(X)**

Group Cash Flow Statement
for the year ended 30th June 2005

	Note	2005 £m
CASH INFLOW FROM OPERATING ACTIVITIES	21	**168.3**
RETURNS ON INVESTMENTS AND SERVICING OF FINANCE		
Interest received		**2.8**
Interest paid		**(7.5)**
NET CASH OUTFLOW FROM RETURNS ON INVESTMENTS AND SERVICING OF FINANCE		**(4.7)**
TAXATION		**(113.8)**
CAPITAL EXPENDITURE AND FINANCIAL INVESTMENT		
Purchase of tangible fixed assets		**(1.9)**
Sale of tangible fixed assets		**2.6**
Disposal/(purchase) of investments: interest in own shares		**1.7**
NET CASH INFLOW/(OUTFLOW) FROM CAPITAL EXPENDITURE AND FINANCIAL INVESTMENT		**2.4**
ACQUISITIONS AND DISPOSALS	22	**83.2**
EQUITY DIVIDENDS PAID		**(55.6)**
CASH INFLOW BEFORE FINANCING		**79.8**
FINANCING		
Issue of ordinary share capital		**7.4**
Decrease in debt due after more than one year	23	**(9.0)**
NET CASH OUTFLOW FROM FINANCING		**(1.6)**
INCREASE IN CASH IN THE YEAR	23	**78.2**

14. CREDITORS DUE WITHIN ONE YEAR

		Group 2005 £m	2004 £m
Bank loans and overdrafts		**4.8**	28.3
Trade creditors (including deferred land payments)		**779.7**	580.9
Amounts due to subsidiary undertakings		**–**	–
Payments on account		**61.6**	32.7
Corporation tax		**60.7**	58.2
Other taxation and social security		**8.3**	5.1
Other creditors		**31.7**	35.8
Accruals and deferred income		**303.8**	289.7
Dividend		**42.8**	35.3
		1,293.4	1,066.0

Movement = £23.5m reduction in overdraft

+

Movement = £54.7m increase in bank and cash

CURRENT ASSETS			
Properties held for sale		**7.2**	9.7
Stocks	12	**2,403.0**	1,977.0
Debtors due within one year	13	**37.7**	41.6
Debtors due after more than one year	13	**2.6**	1.3
Bank and cash		**285.1**	230.4

Figure 5.2 Barratt Developments plc (2005) – Reconciling the cash position

3. *Terminology*

    a. Equity dividends: companies can issue more than one class of share. Preference shares give the holder limited rights but as compensation less exposure to risk should the company encounter difficulties and be forced to close. Equity shareholders have more extensive rights such as voting at company meetings, but their investment carries more risk of loss should the company fail.

b. Liquid resources: These are usually short-term investments that have less than 3 months to maturity when they are acquired. Consequently the cash value is known with a degree of certainty.

c. Treasury bills: Short-term securities issued by the government, and hence carrying negligible risk.

d. Debenture loan: A financial instrument that creates indebtedness owed by the company to the holder of the debenture, usually carrying interest and maturing on a particular date when the principal amount is repaid.

4. *Reconciling the cash position*

The cash flow statement provides an explanation of the movements in the entity's cash position between the beginning and the end of the period (Figure 5.2).

The things every manager must know

1. Cash is the key to short-term viability as profit looks good on paper but it will not pay the bills.

2. Accruals accounting ensures that revenues and associated revenues are reflected in the profit and loss account for the same period thereby giving a true reflection of the profit made on the transaction.

3. A cash flow statement enables a reader to reconcile the opening and closing cash positions of a company by providing a summary of all cash flows for the intervening period.

4. Do not forget that overdrafts are viewed as negative cash.

The Impact of International
Harmonization

The concept of a single GAAP

In recent years, with the development of computer technology and greatly reduced travel times, the World has become a very small place. A potential investor in Australia can simply link into the World Wide Web and within seconds view the financial statements of a public company based in America or France.

Prior to this technological revolution each country had developed its own accounting rule set or GAAP (Generally Accepted Accounting Practice), and rarely had to be concerned about the GAAPs of other countries. This has resulted in divergent presentation of financial information and differing accounting treatments for similar items, but these discrepancies are no longer considered acceptable and there is a groundswell movement towards harmonization. However, this does not imply that the knowledge and skills we learned will become obsolete as the core principles of accounting are generic to every accountant around the globe.

◆ Every transaction has two sides
◆ Accruals accounting is predominant
◆ The accounting equation and concept of articulation are unchanged and so on.

What is the timetable for change?

The champion of accounting change is the IASB (International Accounting Standards Board) whose mission it is to see its IFRS (International Financial Reporting Standards) adopted across the globe. Towards this end huge strides have been taken at the beginning of the 21st century, and for their accounting periods starting on or after 1st January 2005 all listed companies within the European Union that produce group financial statements must prepare those documents in accordance with the international rules. Although this is a massive step towards harmonization it is also a recognition that there cannot be a single point in time when every company switches to the same rules on a single date. Reasons for this stepped approach include:

1. Many countries have indicated their willingness to move over to the new international rules, but logistically need a different time scale.

2. The main emphasis of harmonization is directed towards listed companies. Smaller companies are also being encouraged to make the transfer but the cost to benefit equation is less clear cut. In the UK this issue is being addressed by the progressive adoption of international standards as local rules are updated, but this requires a longer time horizon.
3. The USA and Canada have a close affinity to their own standards which are also of a very high quality. Harmonization with these countries represents the ultimate challenge for the IASB, and they aim to have made significant inroads by 2010.

Presentational differences

If we compare the format of the balance sheet prepared under UK corporate law and accounting standards with the recommendations of the IASB there is one key difference:

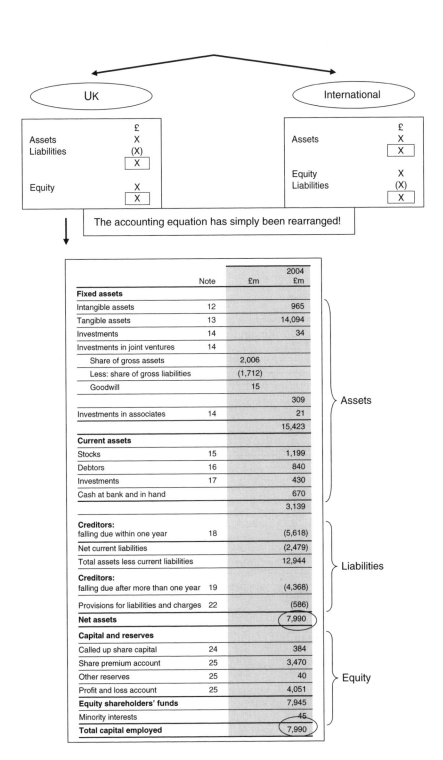

	Note	£m	2004 £m
Fixed assets			
Intangible assets	12		965
Tangible assets	13		14,094
Investments	14		34
Investments in joint ventures	14		
Share of gross assets		2,006	
Less: share of gross liabilities		(1,712)	
Goodwill		15	
			309
Investments in associates	14		21
			15,423
Current assets			
Stocks	15		1,199
Debtors	16		840
Investments	17		430
Cash at bank and in hand			670
			3,139
Creditors: falling due within one year	18		(5,618)
Net current liabilities			(2,479)
Total assets less current liabilities			12,944
Creditors: falling due after more than one year	19		(4,368)
Provisions for liabilities and charges	22		(586)
Net assets			7,990
Capital and reserves			
Called up share capital	24		384
Share premium account	25		3,470
Other reserves	25		40
Profit and loss account	25		4,051
Equity shareholders' funds			7,945
Minority interests			45
Total capital employed			7,990

Illustration 6.1 Tesco plc (2004)

Compare this to the balance sheet of Volkswagon AG (2005)

€ million	Note	Dec. 31, 2005	
Assets			
Noncurrent assets			
Intangible assets	9	7,668	
Property, plant and equipment	10	22,884	
Leasing and rental assets	11	9,882	
Investment property	11	167	
Investments in Group companies accounted for using the equity method	12	4,198	
Other equity investments	12	336	
Financial services receivables	13	24,958	
Other receivables and financial assets	14	2,270	
Deferred tax assets	15	2,872	
		75,235	Assets
Current assets			
Inventories	16	12,643	
Trade receivables	17	5,638	
Financial services receivables	13	22,412	
Current tax receivables	15	317	
Other receivables and financial assets	14	4,856	
Marketable securities	18	4,017	
Cash and cash equivalents	19	7,963	
		57,846	
Total assets		133,081	
Equity and Liabilities			
Equity	20		
Subscribed capital		1,093	
Capital reserves		4,513	
Retained earnings		17,994	Equity
Equity attributable to shareholders of Volkswagon AG		23,600	
Minority interests		47	
		23,647	
Noncurrent liabilities			
Noncurrent financial liabilities	21	31,014	
Other noncurrent liabilities	22	1,591	
Deferred tax liabilities	23	1,622	
Provisions for pensions	24	14,003	
Provisions for taxes	23	2,257	
Other noncurrent provisions	25	5,638	
		56,125	Liabilities
Current liabilities			
Current financial liabilities	21	30,992	
Trade payables	26	8,476	
Current tax payables	23	150	
Other current liabilities	22	6,205	
Other current provisions	25	7,486	
		53,309	
Total equity and liabilities		133,081	

Illustration 6.2 Volkswagon AG (2005)

A move to the USA would find a balance sheet structure that is subtlety different from either of the above. Can you spot the difference?

Box 6.1 Merck & Co Inc. (2005)

($ in millions)

	2005
Assets	
Current Assets	
Cash and cash equivalents	$ 9,585.3
Short-term investments	6,052.3
Accounts receivable	2,927.3
Inventories (excludes inventories of $753.8 in 2005 and $638.7 in 2004 classified in Other assets–see Note 7)	1,658.1
Prepaid expenses and taxes	826.3
Total current assets	21,049.3
Investments	1,107.9
Property, Plant and Equipment (at cost)	
Land	433.0
Buildings	9,479.6
Machinery, equipment and office furnishings	12,785.2
Construction in progress	1,015.2
	23,713.3
Less allowance for depreciation	9,315.1
	14,398.2
Goodwill	1,085.7
Other Intangibles, Net	518.7
Other Assets	6,686.0
	$44,845.8
Liabilities and Stockholders' Equity	
Current Liabilities	
Loans payable and current portion of long-term debt	$ 2,972.0
Trade accounts payable	471.1
Accrued and other current liabilities	5,381.2
Income taxes payable	3,649.2
Dividends payable	830.0
Total current liabilities	13.303.5

Long-Term Debt	5,125.6
Deferred Income Taxes and Noncurrent Liabilities	6,092.9
Minority Interests	2,407.2

Stockholders' Equity
  Common stock, one cent par value
    Authorized–5,400,000.000 shares
    Issued–2,976.223,337 shares–2005

–2,976.230,393 shares–2004	29.8
Other paid-in capital	6,900.0
Retained earnings	37,918.9
Accumulated other comprehensive income (loss)	52.3
	44,901.0

Less treasury stock at cost
  794,299,347 shares–2005

767,591,491 shares–2004	26,984.4
Total stockholders' equity	17,916.6
	$44,845.0

Did you spot that the format is similar to that used under international accounting rules, but the order of the assets is reversed such that they now start with the most liquid (i.e. cash) to the least liquid (i.e. non-current assets).

You will also have spotted that certain items carry a different label under US and international rules to those used under UK GAAP. In particular:

UK	International
Fixed assets	Non-current assets
Stock	Inventory
Debtors	Receivables
Trade creditors	Trade payables
Creditors falling due within year	Current liabilities

The absence of direct reference to greater than or less than one year under international rules is not surprising as they place more emphasis on the concept of the length of the operational cycle – the period between the initiation of a transaction and its completion.

Another difference in terminology is that the profit and loss account as seen in the UK is referred to as the income statement. However, there are only negligible differences in the format of this statement, and these will be dealt with as we analyse the numbers in greater detail.

An example of a cash flow statement prepared under international rules is shown in Box 6.2.

Under international and US rules the format of the cash flow statement is simplified to three key headings.

◆ Operations
◆ Investing
◆ Financing

Additionally unlike a cash flow prepared under UK GAAP it reconciles cash and cash equivalents. The latter are effectively liquid resources which, under UK rules, are one of the reconciling items within the cash flow statement itself.

Box 6.2   Renault S.A. (2004/05) – Cash Flow Statement

€ million	2005	2004[1]
Cash flows from operating activities		
Net income	3,453	2,903
Cancellation of unrealized income and expenses:		
Depreciation and amortization	2,705	2,752
Share in net income (loss) of associates	(2,597)	(1,923)
Dividends received from associates	516	552
Other unrealized income and expenses	393	748
Cash flow	**4,470**	**5,032**
Financing for final customers	(12,998)	(11,917)
Customer repayments	12,485	10,824
Net change in renewable dealer financing	(304)	(35)

Decrease (increase) in Sales Financing receivables	**(817)**	**(1,128)**
Bond issuance by the Sales Financing Division	–	1,100
Bond redemption by the Sales Financing Division	(1,045)	(1,050)
Net charge in other Sales Financing debts	3,119	667
Net charge in other securities and loans of the Sales Financing Division	(39)	227
Net change in Sales Financing financial assets and debts	**2,035**	**944**
Decrease (increase) in working capital	(603)	427
Total	**5,085**	**5,275**
Cash flows from investing activities		
Capital expenditure	(4,018)	(3,923)
Acquisitions of investments, net of cash acquired	(59)	(127)
Disposals of property, plant and equipment and intangibles	1,073	607
Disposals of investments, net of cash acquired, and other	100	34
Total	**(2,904)**	**(3,409)**
Cash flows from financing activities		
Contributions from minority shareholders[2]	(2)	18
Dividends paid to parent company shareholders	(494)	(383)
Dividends paid to minority shareholders	(60)	(35)
Purchases/sales of treasury shares	56	–
Cash flows with shareholders	**(500)**	**(400)**
Bond issuance by the Automobile Division	245	407
Bond redemption by the Automobile Division	(388)	(290)
Net increase (decrease) in other financial liabilities of the Automobile Division[86]	(867)	(998)

Net decrease (increase) in other securities and loans of the Automobile Division	(149)	404
Net change in financial assets and liabilities of the Automobile Division	**(1,159)**	**(477)**
Total	**(1,659)**	**(877)**
Increase in cash and cash equivalents	**522**	**989**
Cash and cash equivalents: opening balance	**5,521**	**4,276**
Increase	522	980
Effect of changes in exchange rates and other changes	108	256
Cash and cash equivalents: closing balance	**6,151**	**5,521**

The things every manager must know

1. The fundamental principles upon which a set of financial statements is prepared is the same irrespective of the country of origin, but there may be changes to format and terminology!

The Managers' Analytical Toolkit

The lull before the storm

To really understand and interpret financial information the well-prepared manager or analyst needs a number of attributes.

- *Commercial knowledge*: Businesses within different commercial sectors produce widely differing financial indicators; without a good knowledge of the sector a wrong diagnosis is easily made.
- *Qualitative skills*: The ability to spot non-financial indicators that provide evidence as to the health of the business.
- *Quantitative skills*: The use of ratios and similar techniques that give measurable criteria against which to benchmark financial position and performance.
- *Accounting choice*: Although there has been drive within the accounting profession to reduce the amount of choice available in the treatment of certain assets and liabilities it has not been eliminated. To compare the performance of one business with another an awareness is needed of these choices and the impact they can have on the figures.

Some of these skills can be easily learned whilst others require the build-up of cumulative knowledge and experience; but our ultimate aim is to combine them all, and this will be the final destination of our progression through analytical skills.

Commercial knowledge

If the figures you are required to review are for the business with which you are directly associated then commercial knowledge should not be a problem, but what if you are looking at the financial data of a competitor or potential acquisition? It is vital that you know the idiosyncrasies of the business sector in which it operates or your interpretation of financial data will potentially be misplaced.

As an example think of a large company that specializes in the construction of residential property.

What are the key business risks?

One of the first steps taken by professional auditors before they begin their review of the financial statements of a client is to identify the risks that face the business. Virtually every business risk has a consequence for the financial numbers.

Example 7.1

Business risk

A company trying to expand into new markets will need additional funding		Levels of debt and ability to pay interest charges will be key areas upon which to focus our analysis

Let us consider what the typical business risks would be for our house construction company.

Business Risk	Financial Implication
Heavy machinery will be required to dig foundations, etc.	These tangible fixed assets will need to be purchased or leased. Both of these alternatives will expose the business to repayment risk.
At any moment in time the company will have large numbers of property in the course of construction.	The company trades in property and hence the uncompleted buildings represent stock and not a fixed asset.
	We would expect a disproportionate amount of working capital to be locked into the least liquid of the current assets. This will influence the marketing strategy of the company as they try to sell from plan or offer financial inducements for early purchase.
Although the company is large it will not be capable of exerting undue pressure over its suppliers as it requires building materials to complete construction which is the priority.	There will be tight cash constraints as cash will tend to leave the business faster than it arrives. Again this may drive the need for longer-term finance.

It is only by understanding these commercial factors that we can direct our other analysis.

Qualitative skills

Many of these are closely aligned to our review of the business risks, and require us to combine information from the non-financial sources contained within the published accounts with commercial factors that impact the business.

Returning to our hypothetical house builder, information that would be of interest to us would include:

◆ The number of new sites acquired
◆ The number of health and safety breaches or accidents in the last year
◆ The number of houses completed
◆ Geographic coverage and any overlap with government initiatives
◆ Any joint ventures or close associations with synergistic entities.

Knowing that the company had been convicted of health and safety breaches would imply that consequential legal action could place stress upon the cash reserves of the business, and in extreme cases this plus the impact on the corporate brand could threaten continuity of operations.

These issues can have a direct impact on a company's ability to stay within financial covenants set by the bank.

Q: What is a financial covenant?

A restriction under which a company must operate in order to borrow money or retain an outstanding loan balance. They take many forms including requiring a company to maintain a minimum cash balance or meeting certain financial ratios – both of which are examples of quantitative measures.

Quantitative measures

Before considering the alternatives allowed by accounting best practice consideration must be given to some of the most noteworthy ratios that will be used to appraise company performance. However, it is important to appreciate that the resultant figures are meaningless on their own as they need to be compared to establish trends or unusual fluctuations and conclusions drawn – they are simply a means to an end and the not the end in itself.

Performance and profitability

◆ $$\text{Gross Margin} = \frac{Net\ Sales - Cost\ of\ Goods\ Sold}{Net\ Sales}$$

This ratio looks at the direct profit made from trading. It uses net sales and hence excludes VAT (value added tax) as this is a tax on the final consumer of the product or service for which the company merely acts as a collection agent on behalf of the government.

Issues:

i. It ignores both administrative overheads and the cost of finance.

◆ $$\text{Operating Profit Margin} = \frac{Operating\ Profit}{Net\ Sales}$$

By including distribution and administrative overheads this ratio highlights operational efficiency. It can prove very effective in highlighting the proportion of overheads that are fixed and the proportion that varies with the scale of operations (more of this later!).

Issues:

i. It ignores the impact of tax and the cost of financing.

◆ $$\text{Net Profit Margin} = \frac{Net\ Profit}{Net\ Sales}$$

This reflects the margin after all expenses have been deducted from profit. Note that dividends are not deducted as they represent an appropriation (i.e. sharing) of profit to the owners of the business rather than an expense.

Issues:

i. The tax expense is normally beyond the control of management as it is set and calculated by government agencies.

Coming attractions: As the impact of differing accounting policies is considered, typical questions that will have to be asked include:

◆ What impact have large one-off items had on the profitability of the business and should they be excluded?
◆ We know that profit and cash are two different concepts and hence might it be useful to strip non-cash items away from profit?

$$\blacklozenge \quad \text{Asset Turnover} = \frac{Net\ Sales}{Average\ Total\ Assets}$$

This ratio shows sales generated per unit of asset, and is often used as a measure of capital intensity – the lower the figure the more intensively the assets are being used. This is useful for comparing the same business between years or for comparison of companies within the same sector.

Remember that the ratio includes total assets and as such includes stock. Hence it can also be a measure of overtrading as companies with this tendency will have low stock figures (i.e. production is struggling to keep pace with demand) and a correspondingly higher asset turnover.

Issues:
    i. A noteworthy problem with this ratio is that it can be very erratic as fixed assets tend to grow in bursts rather than smoothly (e.g. a new office block) whereas turnover has a smoother profile, particularly for large businesses.
    ii. Asset values in the balance sheet are often not reflective of their true worth. This is a subject we will later examine in detail, but a simple analogy is to consider the cost of your home and compare it with the current market price. It is likely that they will differ markedly unless the acquisition was very recent.
    iii. Certain assets will be ignored completely because they have never been valued through purchase, and hence are excluded from the balance sheet. Typically a brand would be an example of such an asset.

$$\blacklozenge \quad \text{Return on Equity} = \frac{Net\ Profit}{Average\ Total\ Equity}$$

This is one of the most used and discussed financial indicators, and note that as with all ratios that draw figures from the profit and loss account and the balance sheet it is usual to average the opening and closing balance sheet position to avoid the distortion of one-off peaks and troughs.

Total equity represents the summation of share capital and all reserves, and the ratio shows the return earned by the company by 'putting these resources to work'. Note that the ratio includes the effects of both finance costs and taxation.

Issues:

i. You will recall that there can be more than one type of share in issue, and this is sometimes exploited to create a variant ratio known as:

$$\text{Return on Ordinary Equity} = \frac{Net\ Profit - Preference\ Dividends}{Average\ Total\ Ordinary\ Equity}$$

This shows the return available to ordinary shareholders after all other deductions. As the name implies preferred share-holders would be paid in preference to ordinary shareholders should the funds of the company run dry.

ii. Return on equity also provides an opportunity to illustrate both the strengths and weaknesses associated with using ration analysis (Figure 7.1).

◆ $\text{Return on Assets} = \dfrac{Net\ Profit}{Average\ Total\ Assets}$

This is a useful ratio for viewing how effectively the assets of the business are being put to work.

Issues:

i. As with many ratios it is important to compare for similar busi-nesses if a meaningful interpretation is to be made. The assets required to operate a car manufacturing plant are obviously very different from those needed for an advertising agency where the greatest asset is its people who are not included on the balance sheet.

◆ $\text{Return on Capital} = \dfrac{Net\ Profit + Gross\ Interest\ Expense}{Average\ Total\ Capital}$

When considering a potential acquisition this is an important ratio, but it is also prone to distortions arising from differences in accounting policy and we will revisit this indicator on numerous occasions.

Issues:

i. When calculating the return on equity and the return on capital employed it is essential not to get the numerator and denomina-tor confused. Total capital includes share capital, reserves and long-term debt, and hence the numerator must include interest as this is the return available to the providers of debt.

Return on equity can be sub-analysed by multiplying the top and bottom of the ratio with sales and total assets.

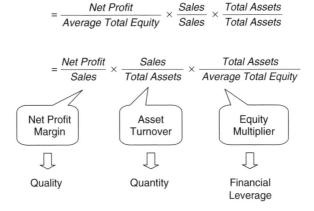

$$\text{Return on Equity} = \frac{\text{Net Profit}}{\text{Average Total Equity}}$$

$$= \frac{\text{Net Profit}}{\text{Average Total Equity}} \times \frac{\text{Sales}}{\text{Sales}} \times \frac{\text{Total Assets}}{\text{Total Assets}}$$

$$= \frac{\text{Net Profit}}{\text{Sales}} \times \frac{\text{Sales}}{\text{Total Assets}} \times \frac{\text{Total Assets}}{\text{Average Total Equity}}$$

| Net Profit Margin | Asset Turnover | Equity Multiplier |
| Quality | Quantity | Financial Leverage |

Figure 7.1 DuPont Analysis

Advantages: By breaking the ratio down into sub-components an insight is gained as to the commercial strategy of the company. A good return could be earned by selling large volumes of product at a modest margin (e.g. supermarket) or by selling fewer items but into a luxury market where higher margins are the norm (e.g. jeweller).

Disadvantages: Unless the management team of a business really understand what drives a ratio then there is not only the opportunity for poor decision-taking, but the creation of an environment for dysfunctional behaviour.

If you were presented with an incentive scheme where bonuses could be earned for improving any of the three components of return on equity which would you choose?

Net Profit Margin: For established goods it is difficult to increase the price of the product in the marketplace, and although cost-cutting is an option to increase margin that might threaten job security.

Asset Turnover: Prices could be cut to increase the volume of sales. This is likely to meet with some measure of success, but if the volume increase is insufficient to mitigate for the reduced selling price this is a strategy that will be difficult to reverse. Your customers will show much greater resistance to an upward restoration of price than they did to the prices being cut.

Additionally the increase in sales will need higher stock levels to service the demand, and in extreme cases new capital assets such as plant and machinery may have to be purchased. This will tend to undermine the asset turnover ratio.

Financial Leverage: The key here is to remember the accounting equation:

$$Assets - Liabilities = Equity$$

If the company borrows when it has no real need for the funds this excess money will remain within the bank; the cash boosting the overall level of assets to match the commensurate increase in liabilities. The impact on the accounting equation is that equity remains unchanged but assets taken in isolation increase leading to an improvement in the financial leverage. You will receive a bonus for your apparent good work, but the position of the company has not improved. In fact the return on equity will fall as the increased interest costs will lower the net profit margin.

Liquidity

◆ $Current\ Ratio = \dfrac{Current\ Assets}{Current\ Liabilities}$

This is the most commonly used liquidity ratio, but is not without its criticisms.

Issues:
   i. Liabilities are settled in cash, but current assets also include debtors and stock. This is not a significant problem if these non-cash items are very liquid.
   ii. Some sources claim that there is a hurdle rate which companies should exceed if they are to remain viable. This rate is stated to be 2:1, but for most industry sectors it is fairly meaningless and should be used with extreme caution.

◆ $Quick\ Ratio = \dfrac{Current\ Assets - Stock}{Current\ Liabilities}$

Also known as the acid test this removes the least liquid of the current assets, and is a better guide to a company's ability to pay.

Before considering other liquidity ratios we should take a moment to introduce the cash conversion cycle (Figure 7.2) as this is the key to understanding a company's liquidity.

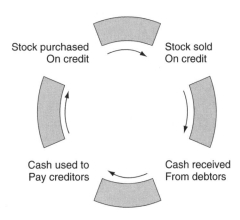

Figure 7.2 The Cash Conversion Cycle

The liquidity ratios which follow allow the components of the cash conversion cycle to be quantified and a vital question to be answered, namely is there a net cash inflow or outflow to/from the business as a result of its operating cycle.

$$\blacklozenge \ \text{Stock Days} = \frac{Average \ Stock}{Cost \ of \ Sales} \times 365$$

This shows the number of days on average an item remains in stock, and will tend to be most accurate when dealing with homogeneous stocks. It is less meaningful for a company with a diverse product range as some items might be selling very quickly whilst others remain on the shelf and become obsolete.

Issues:

i. An alternative to stock days is stock turnover, but it is easy to convert between the two ratios.

$$\text{Stock Turnover} = \frac{Cost \ of \ Goods \ Sold}{Average \ Inventory}$$

$$\text{Stock Days} = \frac{1}{Stock \ Turnover} \times 365$$

Note that the same adjustment can be made to convert the equivalent information for any of the working capital turnover ratios.

◆ Debtor Days $= \dfrac{Average\ Debtors}{Sales} \times 365$

This reflects the average time period for debtors to settle their account, and as such is reflective of the credit controls operated by management. Again the result is very industry-specific, but the basic concept is one familiar to most managers. In how many management meetings have the following parameters been discussed?

- 30 days credit = Ideal
- 45 days credit = Given that many companies settle 1 month after the month in which the invoice is received, this would be deemed to be acceptable
- 60 days credit = Active follow-up of the account
- 90 days credit = Letter warning of imminent legal action

	Total Balance	Current	1 Month	2 Months	3 Months
A Ltd	40,000	30,000	10,000		
B Ltd	17,000				17,000
C Ltd	15,000		5,000	10,000	
D Ltd	550	550			
E Ltd	4,400		2,400	1,200	1,200
F Ltd	80,000	80,000			
G Ltd	60,000		20,000	40,000	
H Ltd	18,000	18,000			
I Ltd	45,000		45,000		
J Ltd	150				150
	£280,500	£128,550	£82,400	£51,200	£18,350

Illustration 7.1 Aged debtor analysis

◆ Trade Creditor Days $= \dfrac{Average\ Trade\ Creditors}{Cost\ of\ Sales} \times 365$

This is the number of days it takes the company to pay its suppliers and, in an ideal world, should approximate to the credit terms they offer, although it is common practice for this to be stretched to ease short-term cash flow.

Issues:

i. This ratio is based on trade creditors and not the summation of all liabilities falling due within one year. This information is rarely provided on the face of the balance sheet and it will be necessary to refer to the notes (Box 7.1).

Box 7.1 Marks & Spencer plc (2004) – Analysis of current liabilities

19. CREDITORS: AMOUNTS FALLING DUE WITHIN ONE YEAR	Group	
	2004 £m	2003 As restated £m
Bank loans, overdrafts and commercial paper[1]	126.0	150.2
Medium-term notes (see note 21B)	216.5	443.9
Securitised loan notes (see note 21B)	2.7	2.5
Trade creditors	210.2	201.6
Amounts owed to Group undertakings	–	–
Taxation	79.8	96.9
Social security and other taxes	43.1	30.5
Other creditors[2]	297.7	288.5
Customer deposits	439.3	78.6
Accruals and deferred income	308.7	270.8
Proposed final dividend	160.7	147.4
	1,884.7	1,710.9

The stock, debtor and creditor day ratios merit further comment when viewed as a whole.

1. It is important that each item of working capital is compared to the correct equivalent from the profit and loss account. Neither stock nor trade creditors include a profit element and hence are compared to the cost of sales whilst debtors do include a profit margin and are compared to sales.
2. To obtain an accurate picture of the working capital dynamics of a business, only credit sales and purchases should be included, but this information is rarely available in the financial statements. However, this does not mean that the ratios should be dismissed as it is trends that are particularly important, and providing the

business has not changed significantly these should still yield useful information. Problems arise when:

a. The company enters new markets or releases new products that differ radically from what has gone before (e.g. a company releases a high-value luxury product where extended credit terms would be the norm).

b. New contracts are signed with major customers or suppliers on new terms.

To ensure you fully understand the significance of the cash conversion cycle, consider Table 7.1.

Table 7.1 The Cash Conversion Cycle	Company A	Company B
Stock days	27	53
Debtor days	38	31
Creditor days	67	72

Which company will have the greater need for long-term borrowing, assuming that both have a similar requirement for capital assets?

Company A – Cash Conversion Cycle

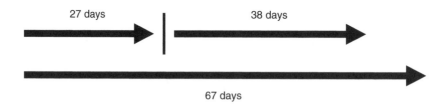

Company B – Cash Conversion Cycle

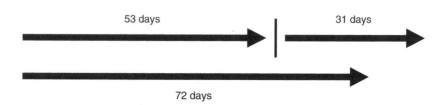

Company A takes 2 days longer to pay its suppliers than the aggregate time that items remain in stock and are then sold and the cash collected. In contrast Company B pays its suppliers 12 days faster than it receives cash in.

Company B will have a greater need for long-term finance as its operations are resulting in a net cash shortfall.

Financial risk ratios

♦ $\text{Gearing} = \dfrac{\text{Long-term Debt}}{\text{Equity}}$

Also known in the US as leverage this shows the proportion of long-term funding that is derived from debt compared to that injected by the owners of the business (i.e. equity). This is a famous ratio often used as a covenant within legal contracts, and highlights one of the classic conundrums for companies, which is to get the balance of this ratio correct. Very few businesses will be funded by equity alone.

Issues:

i. Debt and equity offer both advantages and disadvantages to a business, and these centre around a quote that you may have encountered, but possibly not fully understood.

Debt is cheap

Let us explore this comment further.

	Debt	Equity
Advantage	The interest costs arising on debt are a tax deductible expense, and hence reduce taxable profits. This in turn mitigates physical cash payments made to the tax authorities.	Shareholders (i.e. the providers of equity) are not guaranteed a regular return on their investment. Equity dividends are discretional – and although it may reflect poorly upon the company if payments are not made in times of financial difficulty – it is an option available to management.

Continued

	Debt	Equity
Disadvantage	The providers of long-term finance do not take kindly to breaches in the repayment terms contractually agreed. Effectively interest has to be paid even when the company is facing commercial difficulties.	Dividends are an appropriation (i.e. sharing) of profits rather than an expense against them. Hence they are paid out of profits that have already been subject to taxation, and do not provide a tax shield for the company.

◆ Interest cover $= \dfrac{Profit\ before\ Interest\ and\ Taxation}{Interest\ Expense}$

This provides an indication of the protection available to the providers of finance. The higher the cover the greater the security that their finance costs will be met by the company. A cover of greater than two times is normally considered adequate.

Issues:

i. The fact that a company makes profits that cover the interest due does mean that they have the cash to make the payment.

The things every manager must know

1. Ratio analysis is about comparison and the questioning of results when they do not meet expectations. This can only be accomplished if the user also has a good commercial knowledge of the business sector concerned.
2. Qualitative factors must not be overlooked as they can tell you as much about the business as the financial numbers.
3. A good analyst knows how to break ratios down (e.g. DuPont analysis) or combine them (e.g. cash conversion cycle) to give an increased insight into the performance and position of the company.

The Application of
Knowledge

A basic approach to interpreting the numbers

It would be easy to believe that by calculating a few ratios the answers to all our queries about a business and the financial statements that it produces would be answered – if only this was true!

However, the fact that a larger skills set is required should be perceived as an advantage rather than a drawback. It is the manager who has mastered these skills beyond their peers that can see opportunities and drawbacks not spotted by others, and can add value to a conversation on the direction of the business. These skills will put you one step ahead.

The approach we are about to build will evolve with our skills over the following chapters, and beyond as our own experience grows, but the fundamentals will remain the same. At this stage the model looks very simple (Figure 8.1).

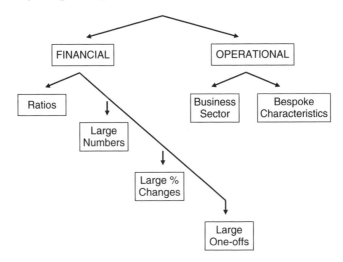

Figure 8.1 **A**nalysis and **I**nterpretation **M**odel for **F**inancial and **O**perational **R**eview [**AIM FOR**]

Operational issues

Picture a large supermarket chain and imagine the answers given by the hypothetical man or woman in the street to the following questions regarding a supermarket:

◆ Are stock levels high?
◆ Do cash reserves represent a large proportion of the assets?

Box 8.1   Wm Morrisons Supermarkets plc – Consolidated balance sheet at 29 January 2006

	Note	2006 £m
Assets		
Non-current assets		
Goodwill and other intangibles	8	–
Property, plant and equipment	9	6,143.9
Lease prepayments	10	217.8
Investment property	11	225.3
Investment in Joint Venture	12	–
Financial assets	101	36.4
		6,623.4
Current assets		
Stocks	14	399.4
Debtors	15	157.4
Cash and cash equivalents	16	135.3
		692.1
Non-current assets classified as held for sale	13	128.6
Liabilities		820.7
Current liabilities		
Creditors	17	(1,471.2)
Other financial liabilities	18	(236.6)
Current tax liabilities		(39.0)
Non-current liabilities		
Other financial liabilities	18	(1,022.7)
Current tax liabilities	21	(422.60)
Pension liabilities	28	(416.2)
Provisions	20	(127.2)
		(1,988.7)
Net assets		3,648.8
Shareholders' equity		
Called up share capital	22	267.3
Share premium	22	36.9
Merger reserve	24	2,578.3
Retained earnings	24	766.1
Total equity		3,648.6

The answer received to both of these questions is likely to be yes, and yet someone with inside knowledge of supermarkets would know that this is not strictly true. As huge corporate entities the amount of stock held appears significant when described in monetary terms, but as a proportion of the balance sheet assets it is less substantial; many stocks are perishable or have legislated sell by dates, which would mean excess supplies would be unsaleable.

Cash balances are also kept in check as the guarantee of more cash arriving at the tills the following day means that cash can be recycled back into stock or long-term financing projects very quickly.

Box 8.1 highlights these observation with stock (5.5%) and cash (1.9%), representing a modest percentage of the gross assets of the company.

The importance of an operational understanding of the business cannot be over-emphasized as without this it is possible to reach conclusions that are at odds with reality. It would not be appropriate to claim that the average supermarket was cash-poor when the reality is that they are cash-rich and very efficient in the utilization of this resource.

Do not ignore the obvious

Micro-analysis of the figures can be very informative, but remember not to become sidetracked and overlook the big changes. The explanation is often obvious, such as a major acquisition or disposal in the year, but think of the knock-on effects you would have expected and be prepared to challenge disparities.

A classic example is exceptional items which are matters that the accountant believes are so material as to warrant separate disclosure either on the face of the profit and loss account or in the notes. Remember these are usually one-off events that may cloud the underlying performance of the business, and you may want to strip them from the figures (Figure 8.2).

	Note	Year ended 30 June 2005		
		Operations, excluding football trading* £'000	Football trading* £'000	Total £'000
Turnover	3	70,550	–	70,550
Operating expenses	4	(57,738)	(12,741)	(70,479)
Operating profit/(loss)	5	12,812	(12,741)	71
Profit/(loss) on disposal of intangible fixed assets	7	–	5,632	5,632
Profit/(loss) on ordinary activities before interest and taxation		12,812	(7,109)	5,703

The effect of the one-off item is sometimes dramatic

Figure 8.2 Tottenham Hotspur plc (2005) – Profit and Loss Account Extract

Case study

Using the skills learnt to date let us examine the figures for our imaginary company Carassius plc, and produce a short management synopsis of its financial position and performance, identifying the further questions we would want to raise.

Carassius Ltd is a long-established food retail chain. In its early days it grew a reputation for the supply of unusual and luxury products with its stores being designed to feel small and intimate. This formula worked well until 2002 when the combined effects of increased competition and a slowing in the growth of the retail sector had a dramatic impact on financial performance.

By 2004 a new management team had been put in place with the skills to stabilize the company and take it forward, including diversification into the supply of premium restaurants that normally pay monthly in arrears for goods ordered. Carassius Ltd was pulled back from the brink of liquidation and produced good trading figures in both the 2005 and 2006 financial years, but to boost growth further the management needed a new strategy if their dreams of ultimately listing the company were to be realized.

Carassius Ltd – Financial extracts

Profit and loss account for the year ended 31 March 2007

Notes		2007 £	2006 £
	Turnover	8,679,894	8,374,886
	Cost of Sales	(7,519,878)	(7,127,564)
	Gross Profit	**1,160,016**	**1,247,322**
	Distribution costs	(137,264)	(128,126)
	Administrative expenses	(461,489)	(481,520)
(1)	**Operating (loss)/profit**	**561,263**	**637,676**
	Interest receivable and similar income	563	910
	Interest payable and similar charges	(16,770)	(21,781)
	Profit on ordinary activities before taxation	**545,056**	**616,805**
	Tax (charge)/credit on profit on ordinary activities	(91,158)	(102,410)
	Profit on ordinary activities after taxation	**453,898**	**514,394**
	Dividends	(75,000)	(25,000)
	(Loss)/profit for the financial year	**378,898**	**489,394**

All operations of the company continued throughout the year and no operations were acquired or discontinued.

Balance sheet as at 31 March 2007

Notes		2007			2006
		£	£	£	£
	Fixed Assets				
	Intangible assets		125,000		–
	Tangible assets		725,390		1,021,320
	Investments		100		100
			850,490		1,021,420
	Current assets				
	Stocks	881,530		619,646	
(2)	Debtors	784,899		333,125	
	Cash at bank and in hand	67,196		202,420	
		1,733,625		1,155,191	
(3)	Creditors: amounts falling due within 1 year	(930,751)		(876,075)	
	Net current assets		802,874		279,116
	Total assets less current liabilities		1,653,364		1,300,536
(4)	Creditors: amounts falling due after more than 1 year		(406,566)		(432,636)
			1,246,798		**867,900**

Notes

Capital and reserves		
Called up share capital	1,000	1,000
Profit and loss account	1,245,798	866,900
Equity shareholders' funds	**1,246,798**	**867,900**

On behalf of the board

NOTE: The figures for 2005 were very similar to 2006 and for ratio analysis purposes can be assumed to be identical.

Selected Notes to the accounts – 30 March 2007

(1) Operating (loss)/profit

(Loss)/profit is stated after charging

	2007 £	2006 £
Depreciation of owned assets	144,820	160,230
Depreciation of leased assets	100,320	107,380
Operating lease rentals	12,215	7,665
Auditors' remuneration in capacity as auditor	48,500	47,000
Loss/(profit) on disposal of fixed assets	1,579	20,475

(2) Debtors

	2007 £	2006 £
Trade debtors	759,189	302,494
Other debtors	19,175	13,253
Prepayments and accrued income	6,535	17,378
	784,899	333,125

(3) Creditors: amounts falling due within 1 year

	2007 £	2006 £
Trade creditors	567,239	509,690
Amounts due to group undertakings	100	100
Obligations under finance leases and hire purchase contract	10,450	10,450
Corporation tax	91,158	102,410
Other taxes and social security	27,107	20,588
Other creditors	28,149	25,888
Dividends	75,000	25,000
Accruals	131,548	181,949
	930,751	876,075

(4) Creditors: amounts falling due after more than 1 year

	2007 £	2006 £
Bank loans	315,000	315,000
Obligations under finance leases and hire purchase contracts	6,512	16,963
Other creditors	75,054	100,673
	406,566	432,636

Key ratios:

♦ $\text{Gross Margin} = \dfrac{Net\ Sales - Cost\ of\ Goods\ Sold}{Net\ Sales}$

2007	2006
$\dfrac{8,679,894 - 7,519,878}{8,679,894} \times 100$	$\dfrac{8,374,886 - 7,127,564}{8,374,886} \times 100$
$= 13.4\%$	$= 14.9\%$

◆ Operating Profit Margin $= \dfrac{Operating\ Profit}{Net\ Sales}$

2007	2006
$\dfrac{561,263}{8,679,894} \times 100 = 6.4\%$	$\dfrac{637,676}{8,374,886} \times 100 = 7.6\%$

◆ Net Profit Margin $= \dfrac{Net\ Profit}{Net\ Sales}$

2007	2006
$\dfrac{453,898}{8,679,894} \times 100 = 5.22\%$	$\dfrac{514,394}{8,374,886} \times 100 = 6.14\%$

◆ Asset Turnover $= \dfrac{Net\ Sales}{Average\ Total\ Assets}$

Note: For the purposes of this analysis the 2005 balance sheet figures can be assumed to be identical to those for 2006.

2007	2006
$\dfrac{8,679,894}{(2,584,115+2,176,611)/2}$	$\dfrac{8,374,886}{(2,176,611+2,094,611)/2}$
$= 3.6$ times	$= 3.8$ times

◆ Return on Equity $= \dfrac{Net\ Profit}{Average\ Total\ Equity}$

2007	2006
$\dfrac{453,898}{(1,246,798+867,900)/2} \times 100$	$\dfrac{514,394}{(867,900+785,900)/2} \times 100$
$= 42.9\%$	$= 59.3\%$

◆ Return on Assets $= \dfrac{Net\ Profit}{Average\ Total\ Assets}$

2007	2006
$\dfrac{453,898}{(2,584,115+2,176,611)/2} \times 100$	$\dfrac{514,394}{(2,176,611+2,094,611)/2} \times 100$
$= 19.1\%$	$= 23.6\%$

◆ Return on Capital $= \dfrac{Net\ Profit + Gross\ Interest\ Expense}{Average\ Total\ Capital}$

2007
$\dfrac{453,898+16,770}{(2,584,115+406,566+2,176,611+432,636)/2} \times 100 = 17.0\%$
2006
$\dfrac{514,394+21,781}{(2,094,611+432,636+2,176,611+432,636)/2} \times 100 = 20.6\%$

◆ Current Ratio $= \dfrac{Current\ Assets}{Current\ Liabilities}$

2007	2006
$\dfrac{1,733,625}{930,751} = 1.86$	$\dfrac{1,155,191}{876,075} = 1.32$

◆ Quick Ratio $= \dfrac{Current\ Assets\ -\ Stock}{Current\ Liabilities}$

2007	2006
$\dfrac{1,733,625-881,530}{930,751} = 0.92$	$\dfrac{1,155,191-619,646}{876,075} = 0.61$

◆ Stock Days $= \dfrac{Average\ Stock}{Cost\ of\ Sales} \times 365$

2007	2006
$\dfrac{(881,530+619,646)/2}{7,519,878} \times 365$	$\dfrac{(619,646+619,646)/2}{7,127,564} \times 365$
$= 36$ days	$= 32$ days

◆ Debtor Days $= \dfrac{Average\ Debtors}{Sales} \times 365$

2007	2006
$\dfrac{(759,189+302,494)/2}{8,679,894} \times 365$	$\dfrac{(302,494+302,494)/2}{8,374,886} \times 365$
$= 22$ days	$= 13$ days

◆ Trade Creditor Days $= \dfrac{Average\ Trade\ Creditors}{Cost\ of\ Sales} \times 365$

2007	2006
$\dfrac{(567,239+509,690)/2}{7,519,878} \times 365$	$\dfrac{(509,690+509,690)/2}{7,127,564} \times 365$
$= 26$ days	$= 26$ days

◆ Gearing $= \dfrac{Long\text{-}term\ Debt}{Equity}$

2007	2006
$\dfrac{406,566}{1,246,798} \times 100 = 32.6\%$	$\dfrac{432,636}{869,900} \times 100 = 49.8\%$

♦ Interest cover $= \dfrac{Profit\ before\ Interest\ and\ Taxation}{Interest\ Expense}$

2007	2006
$\dfrac{561,263+563}{16,770} = 33$ times	$\dfrac{637,676+910}{21,781} = 29$ times

Synopsis

As with all financial analysis it is possible to combine commercial and financial knowledge to understand the dynamics of the company, but it must be remembered that many new questions will arise and explanations sought from management.

It is clear from the figures that the management team have implemented a new strategy, but the early signs are that it has been ill judged.

Performance and profitability

♦ Sales have grown by 3.6 per cent in absolute terms, but this growth appears to have been driven by cutting sales prices as the gross profit margin has fallen. Whilst it is possible that this margin change could be a reflection of a new product mix or higher supplier costs, these seem less likely as the company is operating in a specialized market. This means that mix is more difficult to change plus it is probable that it will have numerous suppliers of bespoke goods and so no single supplier will be able to exert undue influence.
Cutting prices to promote growth is a dangerous policy as customers are delighted when prices fall, but if sale volumes do not mitigate for the price reduction there is always considerable market resistance to prices being pushed back to their original levels.

♦ Operating margins have also fallen, but by a smaller proportion. This is initially surprising as a large proportion of the cost base of this business would be fixed; stores will still consume utilities such as light and heat irrespective of customer numbers, and staff are required to both work the tills and provide customer assistance (remember these are stores that supply luxury goods and the customers will expect good service). However, a closer examination of the profit and loss account shows that tight cost controls have been operated over administrative expenses reversing the expected trend.

It would be useful to quiz management on how these costs have been saved as a reduction in customer service would provide only a short-term gain followed by an erosion of brand with its inevitable knock-on effects.

◆ Net profit margins have tracked operating margins. This is unsurprising as finance costs are immaterial and taxation has dipped with the fall in profits.

It is at this point that the good analyst will think tangentially. We know that the company has overcome some commercial trauma in its recent history and we might want to check that all tax loss relief has been fully exploited.

Another point of interest arises from the trebling of the annual dividend. The notes show that this dividend is unpaid at the year end and this cash flow alone will be sufficient to create an overdrawn position at the bank.

◆ Taken in isolation the asset turnover ratio tells us relatively little although it would be useful to compare this with comparable businesses within the sector to determine if Carassius Ltd is working with its assets more or less effectively to generate revenue.

◆ By contrast the return ratios show a marked decline, and this does give cause for concern. In absolute terms the figures are strong but the rate of deterioration is worrying, particularly as the returns are being squeezed from both sides; profits are falling and assets are being inflated by large increases in working capital.

It should also be remembered that the returns are misleading as the company has recently emerged from severe financial difficulties. On the assumption that it was previously making losses the reserves will have been depleted, leaving equity understated compared to profit following the turnaround. The irony is that if the company had a stable track record the returns would have been lower than those arising from our calculations.

Liquidity

◆ At first glance the liquidity ratios are encouraging as both the current ratio and acid test have improved, but again this is misleading:

 – A reduction in selling prices to promote volume requires additional stocks to meet the anticipated additional sales.
 – Typically most food sales would be for cash although some very wealthy individuals placing large orders may expect credit terms; but the company has diversified to the supply of restaurants on credit and this has driven up year-end debtors.

The true liquidity position is revealed if the cash ratio is calculated.

$$\text{Cash ratio} = \frac{Cash + Cash\ Equivalents}{Current\ Liabilities}$$

2007	2006
$\dfrac{1,733,625 - 881,530 - 784,899}{930,751}$	$\dfrac{1,155,191 - 619,646 - 333,125}{876,075}$
$= 0.07$	$= 0.23$

The deterioration in cash balances to meet immediate working capital demands is now stark.

Working capital

◆ Utilizing the stock, debtor and creditor day figures it is possible to examine the working capital cycle and look more intelligently at the cash position, and anticipate what might happen in the future unless the company changes its policy.

2006

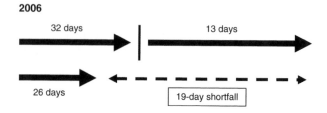

2007

36 days ————————▶ | 22 days ————————▶

26 days ————————▶ ◀ — — — — — —▶
                    [32-day shortfall]

The cash conversion cycle has deteriorated by 13 days which will put increased pressure on the liquidity of the company. The effect of this can be seen in the lower cash position at the balance sheet date in 2007.

Long-term finance

- ◆ The company has not increased its long-term borrowing, but will need to consider this eventuality given the deteriorating cash position. More borrowing will increase the finance cost burden of the company.
- ◆ Interest cover is more than adequate to absorb the increased borrowing but the pressure on cash will build again, being exacerbated by cash interest payments. The company needs to revisit its trading strategy, but this may now be difficult to reverse.
- ◆ Gearing has fallen in 2007, but this has been distorted by a low opening equity position which has increased dramatically in proportionate terms due to the profit made in the year.

Ad hoc

- ◆ It was observed that the company appears to have placed tight controls on administrative overheads, accruals have fallen disproportionately and the question must be asked if the company has window-dressed its financial statements by under-estimating the expenses to be accrued for the year.
- ◆ It would be interesting to discuss with the finance director of Carassius Ltd the nature of 'Other creditors' falling after 1 year as they represent a significant proportion of long-term borrowing; but it is unclear as to what really lies behind the label.

Conclusion

- ◆ Carassius Ltd appears to have adopted a dangerous change to its trading strategy. This has resulted in ratios which give an apparently conflicting picture of its performance and position with some improving whilst others deteriorate.

However, the reality appears to be a company showing early signs of over-trading with increasing stress upon its cash reserves. There are also some worrying indicators that the current management team could be asked some searching questions regarding corporate governance if the distant prospect of a listing became a reality. Questions such as why triple dividends when cash reserves are falling, and were year-end cut-off procedures manipulated to reduce accruals and hence maintain profitability?

If the company is forced to ask for additional long-term funding it is possible that the bank will ask for a fixed or floating charge over the assets, thereby reducing strategic options.

The things every manager must know

1. Analysis does not have to involve complex calculations, it is often a case of looking for large and unusual changes and being able to ask the management team incisive questions rather than vague assertions that can be easily side-stepped.
2. Never look at the numbers in isolation, you must understand the commercial circumstances of the business and the sector in which it operates.
3. Key ratios include:
   a. Gross profit margin
   b. Operating profit margin
   c. Net profit margin
   d. Asset turnover
   e. Return on equity
   f. Return on assets
   g. Return on capital
   h. Current ratio
   i. Acid test
   j. Cash ratio
   k. Stock days
   l. Debtor days
   m. Creditor days
   n. Gearing
   o. Interest cover.

Investor Analysis

The investment decision and why it matters

When considering the use of investor ratios one of two images usually comes to mind.

1. A small investor using the pages of the financial press to review the performance of companies with a view to buying shares as part of a small personal portfolio.
2. A large predatory company reviewing the financial statistics of a potential target.

In both of these cases the emphasis is upon a third party, but there is another possibility that occurs so frequently that it is often forgotten. As companies grow they need cash to finance this expansion, and it is rare that trading operations alone will be sufficient to provide these funds. Irrespective of whether this cash is derived from borrowing or the issue of additional equity (i.e. shares), it is in the interests of management to make the finances of the business look attractive to encourage this investment.

As an analyst of financial data it is important that you are aware of the key financial indicators used to appraise the potential of an investment as by so doing you can place yourself in the minds of management and consider how they might be tempted to window-dress the numbers.

Although the ratios considered can be calculated for any company they are principally relevant for listed companies who have a wide shareholder base.

Earnings per share

This is a widely available ratio and listed companies are required to disclose earnings per share (EPS) details at the foot of the profit and loss account (Figure 9.1).

There is a requirement to disclose two versions of EPS, but many companies will include additional variants they believe highlight useful information to the reader of the financial statements. However, this additional information cannot be disclosed more prominently than the two required as best practice by accounting standards – these are referred to as the basic and diluted EPS respectively.

EPS Disclosures

> The term income statement is the international equivalent to the profit and loss account

Group income statement

For the 52 weeks ended 30 September 2006

	Notes	2006 52 weeks Before exceptional items £m	Exceptional items* £m	Total £m
Revenue	1, 2	1,720	–	1,720
Operating costs before depreciation and amortisation	3, 8	(1,290)	(7)	(1,297)
Profit arising on property-related items	8	–	23	23
EBITDA**		430	16	446
Depreciation and amortisation	13, 14	(121)	–	(121)
Operating profit	2	309	16	325
Finance costs	8, 9	(118)	(4)	(122)
Finance revenue	9	9	–	9
Net finance income from pensions	9	8	–	8
Profit before tax		208	12	220
Tax expense	8, 10	(64)	39	(25)
Profit for the financial period attributable to equity holders of the parent		144	51	195
Earnings per ordinary share				
Basic	12	29.3p		39.7p
Diluted	12	28.6p		38.8p

Figure 9.1 Mitchells & Butlers plc (2006)

$$\blacklozenge \; \text{Basic EPS} = \frac{Earnings}{Weighted\ Average\ Number\ of\ Ordinary\ Shares}$$

It should be noted that EPS is based on ordinary shares only, and it is important that these can be distinguished from preference share capital.

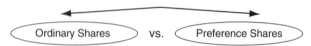

Ordinary Shares   vs.   Preference Shares

◆ Ordinary shares usually carry a right to vote whereas for preference shares there is no such right unless dividend payments fall into arrears

◆ If a company is wound up preference share holders rank above ordinary share holders, but are usually repayable at their par value

◆ Dividends on ordinary shares are variable (i.e. dependent upon company performance) whereas preference dividends are usually fixed.

Earnings per share uses the weighted average number of shares for the period as a company may issue additional share capital or repurchase shares in the period, and these changes need to be reflected.

The earnings figure represents profit after the deduction of all expenses including interest and taxation, and after the deduction of preference dividends as these would be paid in advance of their ordinary share equivalent.

Diluted EPS serves a different purpose as it acts as an early warning sign for changes that might lie ahead – namely the existence of financial instruments that could lead to a future increase in the number of ordinary shares and a consequential reduction in the EPS as earnings are spread more thinly. There are three potential diluting factors:

1. *Convertible debt*: This is a debt instrument that allows the holder to convert the debt into ordinary shares at a future date.
2. *Convertible preference shares*: Remember that EPS is based exclusively on ordinary shares and hence would exclude the preference shares until conversion.
3. *Options*: These entitle the holder to buy shares at a stipulated price at a future date, and in reality would only be exercised if the market price of the shares exceeded the exercise price of the option so that an instant profit could be realized. There would be no point in paying to exercise an option if shares were trading at below the exercise price as it would be cheaper for the holder to buy shares directly on the market.

The diluted EPS always assumes the worse-case scenario by anticipating that all options will be exercised, all debt converted and so on.

As previously mentioned it is common for companies to include additional versions of EPS that they consider will be helpful to a user of the financial statements (Figure 9.2)

	Pence
Earnings per share 10	
Underlying	10.6
Basic	12.1
Diluted	11.7

> This excludes exceptional one-off gains so that a reader gets a clearer picture of the on-going earnings of the company

Figure 9.2 Somerfield plc (2005) – EPS variants

The price–earnings ratio

This is one of the most widely used measures for comparing companies within the same business sector.

$$\blacklozenge \ \text{P/E ratio} = \frac{Share\ Price}{Earnings\ per\ share}$$

Effectively this gives the number of years it would take to earn the company's current market value, assuming the current earning power is sustained. At its simplest it is a measure of confidence in the future performance of the company, and companies with a higher P/E ratio would be preferred to their competitors as an investment opportunity.

However, as with all ratios it is possible to misinterpret the signals unless you think beyond a bland acceptance of the numerical result. Consider the following:

- ◆ A poorly performing company may have an unexpectedly high P/E ratio if the markets are aware of a takeover bid, offering a high price because they perceive synergistic benefits in the future.
- ◆ A company is known to be investing heavily to create future growth. In the light of this knowledge the share price rises, but the new investment has not yet had time to generate additional earnings. This leads to an inflated P/E ratio.
- ◆ A company with strong current earnings has failed to invest in its capital structure for the future. The financial markets are aware of this under-investment and the share price falls in advance of the anticipated deterioration in earnings. The P/E ratio will be understated.

P/E ratios are often discussed in the same breath as yields, and this is a relationship that we need to understand!

Dividend yields

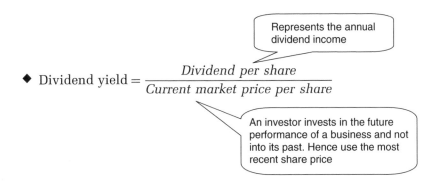

- Dividend yield = $\dfrac{Dividend\ per\ share}{Current\ market\ price\ per\ share}$

> Represents the annual dividend income

> An investor invests in the future performance of a business and not into its past. Hence use the most recent share price

---

A technical moment!

Most companies pay two dividends in a year referred to as the interim and final; but, with changes made to accounting practice, care is needed in the identification of the correct dividend to be used in the yield calculation.

The rules say that a dividend can only be recognized as an appropriation in the financial statements if it was declared within the financial year. This is not a problem for the interim dividend as it usually falls in the middle of the accounting period, but final dividends are declared after the balance sheet date when the financial performance and position of the business have been finalised.

Let us consider the repercussions:

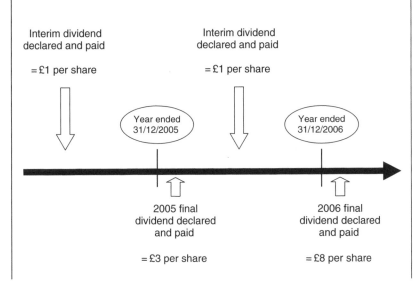

Interim dividend declared and paid = £1 per share

Interim dividend declared and paid = £1 per share

Year ended 31/12/2005

Year ended 31/12/2006

2005 final dividend declared and paid = £3 per share

2006 final dividend declared and paid = £8 per share

In the 2006 financial statements dividend appropriations will comprise the 2005 final dividend and the 2006 interim dividend as these were declared and paid in the year ended 31 December 2006. The 2006 final dividend will be disclosed by way of note as the shareholders will want to be aware of this information, but this appropriation will be deducted from the reserves in 2007 when it was declared and paid.

An investor wants to know about the current dividend policy of the company and not that of a previous year. The differences are potentially dramatic as can be seen if we assume that the current market price of a share was £24 at 31 December 2005 and £35 at 31 December 2006.

- 2006 [based on date dividend paid] $\dfrac{£3 + £1}{£35} \times 100 = 11.4\%$

- 2006 [based on dividends proposed] $\dfrac{£8 + £1}{£35} \times 100 = 25.7\%$

The correct yield is 25.7%.

If appraising the justification of an investment by comparison to other alternatives the disparity shown above could lead to a seriously flawed investment appraisal.

High P/E ratios are often associated with low yields. A high P/E ratio suggests confidence in the company and an expectation of growth in the future. A low yield suggests funds are being retained within the business for capital growth. It should be noted that the relationship between the P/E ratio and the yield is inverse such that a high P/E ratio suggests similar objectives to a low dividend yield.

Do not forget that an unquestioning acceptance of any financial indicator is dangerous. Can you spot a potential flaw in using dividend yields?

YES: Dividend payments on ordinary shares are at the discretion of management and hence a change in yield might not suggest an improvement or deterioration in the underlying business but simply a change in management strategy.

Other useful indicators

Dividend cover

◆ $\text{Dividend cover} = \dfrac{Earnings\ per\ share}{Dividend\ per\ share}$

This ratio can be used to assess the ability of a company to sustain its current level of dividend, but it is undermined by the same key weakness as all indicators centred on dividends, namely their discretionary nature. When surveying the numbers you must also ensure that the cash position is considered as it is not profit that pays the dividend but cash.

A dividend cover in excess of 2 is considered comfortable, but if this figure falls below 1 it requires some serious questions to be asked as the company is distributing in excess of the profits made for the year and hence will be eating into the accumulated reserves brought forward from previous periods.

One interesting variation for this indicator is to invert the ratio

◆ $\text{Payout ratio} = \dfrac{Annual\ Dividend\ per\ share}{Earnings\ per\ share}$

The payout ratio highlights the proportion of earnings being appropriated to shareholders. There is no right or wrong solution, but consideration must be given to the ambitions of investors, and the balance they require between immediate investment revenues and capital growth. Investors interested in the latter would prefer a low payout ratio so that the funds can be directed into the capital infrastructure of the business, acquisitions, new product launches and so on. These individuals are often already subject to a high tax burden and do not want to increase it further.

> **Variations on a theme:**
>
> The payout ratio is often used to calculate the retention rate.
>
> $Retention\ rate = 1 - Payout\ ratio$
>
> This is simply looking at the same information from another perspective.

Net asset value

♦ $\text{Net asset value} = \dfrac{\textit{Net assets}}{\textit{Number of ordinary shares in issue}}$

This is an indicator that must be used with caution as it shows the theoretical amount shareholders would receive if the company were to be liquidated. However, it assumes that all the assets and liabilities will be realised or settled at exactly the values shown in the balance sheet – this is very unlikely.

1. Some assets, such as property, will often have market values in excess of their balance sheet value.
2. Some assets will not be reflected on the balance sheet (e.g. brand values).
3. New liabilities will be incurred when a company is liquidated – typically redundancy and similar costs associated with employee contract severance.

The things every manager must know

1. Investor ratios are relevant primarily to listed companies.
2. Earnings per share (EPS) looks at earnings exclusively on ordinary shares.
3. Diluted EPS reflects the maximum reduction in EPS that would occur if all convertible instruments and options in existence were exercised. It is an early warning indicator of the worst-case scenario.
4. Ratios analysing dividends must be treated with caution because of their discretionary nature.

Cash Ratios

The ability to pay

We have already established that profit and cash are two completely separate issues, and when a financial institution is considering lending money to a company its most important consideration is the ability to pay.

This does not mean that the ratios considered so far are obsolete as the bank will want to confirm that its customer has a viable business, but it does infer that some additional indicators with an emphasis exclusively on cash are required. The significance of cash has long been recognized and more than 40 years ago W.H. Beaver showed that comparing cash flows to total debt was a strong indicator of potential corporate failure.

The cash recovery rate

◆ Cash recovery rate $= \dfrac{Cash\ flow\ from\ operations}{Average\ gross\ assets} \times 100$

Rather confusingly it is usual for the cash flows from operations to include the proceeds arising from the disposal of long-term assets.

This ratio shows the rate at which a company recovers its investment in assets with a faster recovery rate implying lower risk. As with all cash-based ratios this is more difficult for a creative finance director to manipulate as cash balances are a factual number easily validated by reference to a bank statement.

Cash return on capital employed

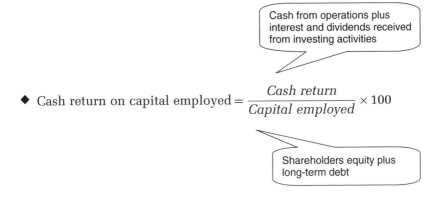

Cash from operations plus interest and dividends received from investing activities

◆ Cash return on capital employed $= \dfrac{Cash\ return}{Capital\ employed} \times 100$

Shareholders equity plus long-term debt

It is vital that we appreciate one of the key differences between this ratio and the profit-based return on capital employed. The latter includes a number of non-cash expenses such as depreciation of fixed assets which, as we shall see in later chapters, can be easily manipulated by a skilled accountant.

Cash interest cover

♦ Cash interest cover $= \dfrac{Cash\ return}{Interest\ PAID}$

Subject to renegotiation with the bank, interest payments cannot be avoided as there is a contractual obligation to pay. This ratio gives a clear indicator of the business to meet these payments with any shortfall in cash return leading to a depletion of cash reserves.

It should be noted that if cash reserves fall there is a danger of creating a vicious circle in which a company needs to borrow so that financing costs can be paid, but this results in higher interest payments.

Cash dividend cover

This represents the cash return as used for cash interest cover less payments made in respect of interest and tax

♦ Cash dividend cover $= \dfrac{Cash\ flow\ available\ for\ ordinary\ shareholders}{Equity\ dividends\ paid}$

If the cash dividend cover exceeds 1 this indicates that the business is generating sufficient cash from operations and investments, after paying off finance charges, to allow for a dividend.

Looking beyond the financial pages

The purpose of this text is to introduce you to mechanisms by which financial information is produced and facilitate your ability to interpret it in a way that enhances decision-making. However, it is occasionally useful to stand back and look at the overlap between these skills and other aspects of the corporate world. In relation to cash two such overlaps are particularly noteworthy.

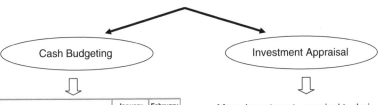

	January	February
Sales	3000	1500
Other Income	2000	500
TOTAL Income for the Month	5000	2000
Creditors	2000	3000
Other Payments	1700	2100
Purchase/Hire of Fixed Assets	2000	500
TOTAL Payments for the Month	5700	5600
Opening Balance at Month Start	4000	3300
Add Total Income for the Month	5000	2000
Less Total Payments for the Month	5700	5600
BANK BALANCE at Month End	3300	(300)

Unlike financial statements that are fundamentally based on historic information, a cash budget has an exclusively forward-looking perspective.

They require the extensive use of estimates and judgement. Consequently such prospective financial information tends to make accounting professionals very nervous.

Many investment appraisal techniques focus on future cash flows.

A simple example is payback which looks at the time it will take for an investment to generate cash flows sufficient to cover the initial outlay.

One problem with this technique is that unless adjusted it ignores the fact that in times of positive inflation (i.e. the usual state of affairs) the purchasing power of money erodes with time, but this is a discussion for another day.

The things every manager must know

1. Unlike most figures included within a set of financial statements the cash position is difficult to manipulate as it represents a balance that can easily be validated by an independent third party, namely the bank.
2. Important cash-based ratios include:
   ◆ Cash recovery rate
   ◆ Cash return on capital employed
   ◆ Cash interest cover
   ◆ Cash dividend cover.

Getting to Grips with
Accounting Choice

Why choice matters

Imagine that your employer has just purchased an overseas company, and in the footnote to the announcement sent to all staff are the following details:

Key statistics	
Return on capital employed	
Parent Company	Overseas Acquisition
14.3%	9.1%
Gearing	
Parent Company	Overseas Acquisition
31.9%	38.2%

Initially the acquisition appears to be a strange decision by senior management as the overseas investment has higher gearing and a poorer return on capital. Unless the acquisition was made because synergistic effects are expected to accrue in the future it appears as if those in charge have lost the plot!

All is not as it first appears and examination of the accounting policies of the two companies highlights an interesting difference. The overseas operation has a policy of regularly revaluing its properties to their current market value, which is significantly in excess of their original cost. By contrast the parent company does not revalue.

We shall examine the balance sheet and think through the logic of a company increasing the carrying value of its property portfolio:

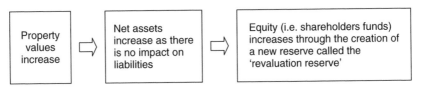

These consequences can be summarized as follow (Figure 11.1).

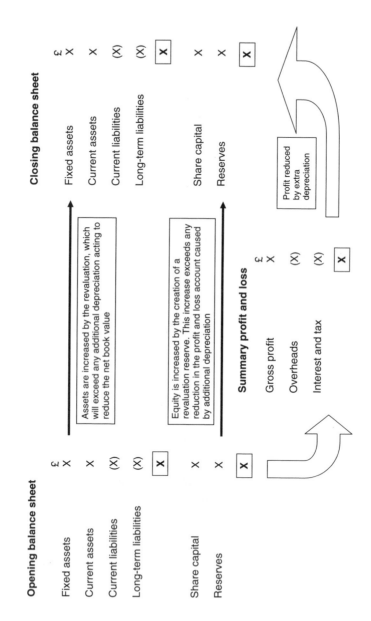

Figure 11.1 The impact of differing accounting policies

If the accounting policies of the acquired company are brought into line with those of the parent company the value of assets and equity will fall as the carrying value of the asset is reduced to depreciated cost. Simultaneously annual depreciation expenses will fall, and the net consequence will be to improve the financial statistics that had originally caused us concern.

By eliminating the revaluation the return on capital improves and gearing falls

- Return on Capital $= \dfrac{Net\ Profit + Gross\ Interest\ Expense}{Average\ Total\ Capital}$

Debt is unchanged

- Gearing $= \dfrac{Long\text{-}term\ Debt}{Equity}$

The origin of choice

The rules that govern the preparation of financial statements are often referred to as generally accepted accounting practice (GAAP), and this comprises of several facets.

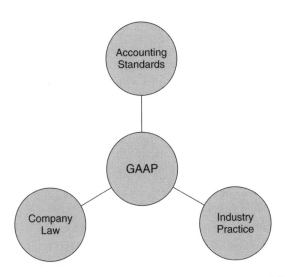

In the UK accounting standards are referred to as Financial Reporting Standards (FRS), although a few standards remain from an earlier era and carry the label SSAP (Statement of Standard Accounting Practice).

The GAAP of other countries will potentially differ from that of the UK, and in spite of a drive for global harmonization this target has yet to be realized – although the International Accounting Standards Board (IASB) have made huge strides towards this end.

The UK Companies Act gives considerable guidance on:

◆ Disclosure rules
◆ Financial statement formats
◆ Valuation issues.

Outside of the lofty circles of the accounting profession the 'labels' designated by standards and law are relatively unimportant, but the key principles and choices they contain are the very life blood of a reviewer/analyst.

What has this business done?

To answer this question we must look to the accounting policies note which is usually note 1 to any set of financial statements (Box 11.1).

The policies should give clarification of the accounting approach adopted for all the key numbers within the accounts. Typical subjects covered include:

◆ Tangible fixed assets
◆ Intangible fixed assets
◆ Leased assets
◆ Revenue recognition
◆ Foreign exchange
◆ Methods used in the preparation of group financial statements
◆ Stocks
◆ Finance costs
◆ Taxation.

Remember that directors of the company are expected to run the business in the best interests of its investors, and produce financial statements that reflect a true and fair view to this key stakeholder group. However, do not blindly accept the information presented to you as an embodiment of the truth.

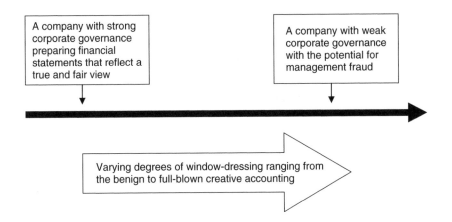

A company with strong corporate governance preparing financial statements that reflect a true and fair view

A company with weak corporate governance with the potential for management fraud

Varying degrees of window-dressing ranging from the benign to full-blown creative accounting

Box 11.1 Tottenham Hotspur plc (2005) – Extract from accounting policies

1. Accounting policies

The following accounting policies have been applied consistently by the Directors in both the current and preceding periods in dealing with items which are considered material in relation to the Group's accounts.

Basis of accounting

The accounts have been prepared in accordance with applicable United Kingdom accounting standards and under the historical cost convention with the exception that certain freehold and leasehold properties have been revalued.

Basis of consolidation

The consolidated accounts incorporate the accounts of Tottenham Hotspur plc and its subsidiaries. A separate Profit and Loss Account dealing with the results of the Company only has not been presented as permitted by Section 230 of the Companies Act 1985.

Turnover

Turnover represents income receivable from football and related commercial activities, exclusive of VAT.

Gate receipts and other matchday revenue is recognised as the games are played. Sponsorship and similar commercial income is recognised over the duration of the respective contracts. The fixed element of broadcasting revenues is recognised over the duration of the football season whilst facility fees received for live coverage or highlights are taken when earned. Merit awards are accounted for only when known at the end of the football season.

Signing-on fees and loyalty payments

Signing-on fees are charged evenly, as part of operating expenses, to the Profit and Loss Account over the period of the player's contract.

Loyalty fees are accrued, as part of operating expenses, to the Profit and Loss Account over the period to which they relate.

Grants receivable

Grants receivable are credited to a deferred credit account and released to the Profit and Loss Account over the estimated useful life of the asset in respect of which they are receivable.

Foreign exchange

Transactions denominated in foreign currencies are translated into sterling and recorded at the rates of exchange ruling at the date of the transactions. Monetary assets and liabilities denominated in a foreign currency are translated into sterling at the exchange rates ruling on the Balance Sheet dates. Translation differences are dealt with in the Profit and Loss Account.

Intangible fixed assets

The costs associated with the acquisition of players' and key football management staff registrations are capitalised as intangible fixed assets. These costs are fully amortised over their useful economic lives, in equal annual instalments over the period of the respective contracts. Player's registrations are written down for impairment when the carrying value exceeds the amount recoverable through use or sale and the reduction in value is considered permanent.

Profits or losses on the disposal of these registrations represent the consideration receivable, net of any transaction costs, less the unamortised cost of the original registration.

Tangible fixed assets

Freehold land is not depreciated. Leasehold property is amortised over the term of the lease. Other fixed assets are depreciated on a straight line basis at annual rates appropriate to their estimated useful lives as follows:

Freehold properties	2%–4%
Motor vehicles	20%
General plant and equipment	10%–33%

The things every manager must know

1. Understanding the legitimate choices made by a business as allowed by accounting standards is a key skill in evaluating and comparing the financial statements of companies.
2. The term 'generally accepted accounting practice (GAAP)' represents the suite of guidance, legal and professional, by which financial statements are prepared.
3. GAAP may vary from country to country, but there is a drive towards global harmonization.

Tangible Fixed Assets

What constitutes a tangible fixed asset?

In earlier chapters we established that tangible fixed assets share several common features.

- ◆ They have physical substance
- ◆ They are for long-term use within the business and expected to generate future benefits (e.g. facilitate the production of stock)
- ◆ They are not actively traded although a business will buy and sell such assets as they wear out or as the business grows.

Tangible fixed assets take many forms.

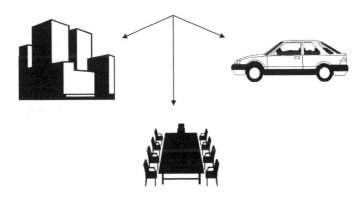

Various labels are sometimes associated with this type of asset, and hence be on your guard for:

L&B   Land and buildings
PPE   Property, plant and equipment

It is because that they are often items with which we are familiar that many see little accounting danger in these assets, but to a creative finance director they represent a golden opportunity for them to manipulate the financial statements.

Fixed or not?

When looking at a large industrial warehouse there is little doubt that it is a fixed asset of the business, but not all decisions are this clear cut.

Materiality: Businesses will often purchase numerous small assets that are not for resale. These could include tools, pallets and desk stationery such as hole punches. The monetary amounts are not material to the financial statements and to avoid creating unnecessary accounting complications they are expensed directly against profit.

Established practice: Some industries have established practices that although not in line with expectations have become the norm. If such practice is used consistently between accounting periods it has a minimal distorting impact on the figures.

Future benefits: These may not always be clear and hence divergent opinions arise over the treatment of the associated item. A good example would be environmental and safety equipment not specifically required by law. The purchaser may get a future benefit in terms of enhanced reputation but this is difficult to quantify.

Hopefully you have already spotted what will become a recurrent theme associated with many areas of accounting practice. There are many areas of choice and interpretation, and it is the impact of the choices made by management that we must understand if we are to understand the real story behind the financial information they produce.

Identifying cost

It would be reasonable to assume that the cost of a fixed asset was simply the figure at the bottom of the purchase invoice. Sadly this might be reasonable, but it is not always the case!

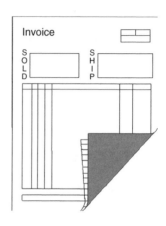

Import duties and non-refundable purchase taxes are added to the purchase together with all direct costs needed to bring the asset to its current location and condition. This includes costs needed to bring the asset into normal use such as the connection fee to utilities without which the asset will not function.

Management often focus on ensuring good news today and worry less about the future knock-on effects. Consequently it is in their interests to roll expenses into the carrying value of the asset and hence maintain profits. We will need to look at this again as it has been the theme of many corporate frauds.

The concept of depreciation

'Depreciation' is a term that has already been used several times within this text, and on each occasion my guess is that you nodded quietly to yourself acknowledging that this was a term with which you felt comfortable, but all may not be as it seems.

It would be easy to believe that subsequent to its acquisition an asset falls in value through use and technological obsolescence, and that depreciation is simply a measure of the amount by which the value has fallen, but technically this is not correct.

| Asset cost | less | Depreciation since acquisition | $\neq$ | Current value |

There are two major reasons for this disparity.

1. Asset values do not always fall, and in a later section we will consider the impact of an upward revaluation.
2. Depreciation is a mechanism that matches the cost of the asset to the period over which benefit is gained from its use, and although this may approximate to its value it is not reflection of the amount that would be realized in the open market.

Depreciation mechanics

The most common method for calculating depreciation is known as the straight-line method.

◆ Annual depreciation charge $= \dfrac{Cost - Estimated\ Residual\ Value}{Estimated\ Useful\ Economic\ Life}$

The basic accounting for this charge is shown in Example 12.1, but immediately the dangers of depreciation are clear as both the useful economic life of the asset and its residual value at the end of this period are estimates. This provides scope for manipulation by management (e.g. a doubling of the useful economic life halves the expense and increases profit, asset values and equity which will have a beneficial impact on key ratios).

It is this discretionary element to depreciation and the fact that it does not create a cash flow that leads many analysts to exclude it from the numbers. This is the origin of the term EBITDA (Earnings before interest, tax, depreciation and amortization).

Example 12.1

Accounting for depreciation

ABC plc purchases new plant and machinery for £25,000 and estimates that it was to make a valuable contribution to the business for 5 years after which it can be sold for £5,000.

◆ Annual depreciation charge $= \dfrac{25{,}000 - 5000}{5} = £4{,}000$ per annum

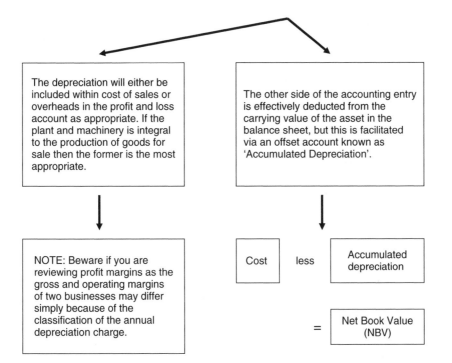

Year	Depreciation Expense £	Accumulated Depreciation £	Net Book Value £
Start			25,000[Cost]
1	4,000	4,000	21,000
2	4,000	8,000	17,000
3	4,000	12,000	13,000
4	4,000	16,000	9,000
5	4,000	20,000	5,000

Residual value

Depreciation – further choice

There are numerous approaches to the calculation of depreciation, and this is a classic example when reference to the accounting policies of the company can provide some useful pointers.

(ii) Depreciation

Depreciation of property, plant and equipment is provided to reflect a reduction from cost to estimated residual value over the estimated useful life of the asset to the Group. Depreciation of property, plant and equipment is calculated using the straight-line method and the annual rates applicable to the principal categories include:

Freehold and long leasehold buildings	– between 2% and 5%
Short leaseholds	– over remaining period of the lease
Tenants' fixtures	– between 5% and 25%
Computers and electronic equipment	– between 25% and 50%
Motor cars	– 25%
Commercial vehicles	– between 10% and $33^1/_3$%

Freehold land is not depreciated.

Illustration 12.1 Kingfisher plc (2005/06) – Accounting policy extract

Straight line is undoubtedly the common method of depreciation, but there are several other methods which are described as accelerating depreciation because they generate a higher charge in the early years on an asset's life. Such methods tend to be used for assets such as motor vehicles, which are known to fall dramatically in value from the moment they are driven from the showroom.

Some of the most frequently used methods of accelerated depreciation are

- The reducing balance method
- Sum of digits
- Double declining balance (principally used in USA).

As a reviewer we can leave the details of the calculations to the accounting professionals whilst we concentrate on the impact they have on the reported figures, and why management might select a particular approach.

The following table shows the impact of straight line and accelerated methods in the first year following the acquisition of the asset.

Table 12.1 Straight line vs. accelerated depreciation		
Variable	Straight line	Accelerated
1 Profits	Higher	Lower
2 Shareholders' equity	Higher	Lower
3 Cash flow	Same	Same
4 Liquidity ratio	Same	Same
5 Debt-to-equity	Lower	Higher
6 Return to equity	Higher	Lower

1. In the early years accelerated methods are more prudent and reduce profits.
2. If profits are reduced there is less to transfer to reserves at the period end and as a consequence equity is lower compared to when straight-line methods are used.
3. Depreciation is an accounting entry – no cash is received or paid.
4. Liquidity ratios such as the acid test are independent of depreciation which has no impact on cash, and lowers the carrying value of fixed assets not current assets.
5. By lowering shareholders equity accelerated depreciation techniques worsen gearing as the level of long-term debt remains unchanged.
6. Accelerated depreciation initially reduces profits and hence depresses both returns and equity, but in proportional terms if the reduction in profit is greater this performance indicator deteriorates.

The fact that the estimates and methods used for depreciation are at the discretion of management highlights the scope for massaging of the numbers. When comparing two busi esses in the same sector you should always be asking questions such as:

◆ Which method of depreciation is being used and has it been used consistently?
◆ If accelerated methods are being used, are the assets recently acquired or close to the end of their useful economic life (remember that this method is very prudent initially, but actually boosts

performance in the latter years as the value of the asset has been substantially reduced)?

♦ Have any of the estimates such as useful economic life been changed?

Depreciation ratios

There are several ratios associated with depreciation, but as we shall observe they must be used with caution.

♦ Average Age of Fixed Assets $= \dfrac{Accumulated\ Depreciation}{Annual\ Depreciation\ Expense}$

♦ Remaining Asset Life $= \dfrac{Net\ Book\ Value}{Annual\ Depreciation\ Expense}$

These ratios only give meaningful results when:

1. The method of depreciation is straight line
2. The residual value is nil
3. Estimates have not been changed over the life of the asset.

If the above do not apply then a misleading picture is obtained of the fixed asset portfolio.

Revaluation

With the exception of antiques or vintage status the value of fixtures and fittings or motor vehicles will fall over time, but the same is not true of property. The value of the latter has risen inextricably over recent decades with short-term slumps being recouped and surpassed. As a reviewer we must understand if the continued depreciation of such assets is appropriate, and decide if gains in value can be reflected in the financial statements.

Cast your mind back to the description of depreciation we previously identified. Remember that it is a method of allocating cost to the periods which can benefit from the use of the assets – it is not about adjusting the carrying value of the asset to its current market value.

All fixed assets should be depreciated irrespective of whether their market value rises or falls. The one exception is land which has an infinite life such that annual depreciation is effectively nil.

However should the continued depreciation of a fixed asset mean that increases in its market value should be ignored? The answer to this question partially depends on the accounting regime being used.

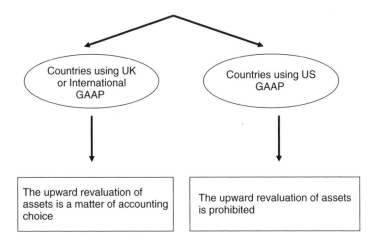

When upward revaluation is allowed and management decide to adopt this approach it must be done consistently, and cherry picking is not permitted. This means that the decision to revalue is taken by class of asset (e.g. all properties) rather than simply selecting those assets that have increased in value the most to enhance the financial statements.

When the opportunity to increase asset value exists you might assume that this would be grasped by the management team as an easy way to improve the balance sheet, but in reality this opportunity is not always taken. Put yourself in the position of the management . . .

◆ Increased asset values will lead to increased annual depreciation charges. If it is important for you to maximise profits then revaluation will seem less attractive.

◆ It is rare that a company will reflect current values for other assets on the balance sheet (e.g. stock), and so by revaluing some fixed assets the balance becomes a mishmash of values that is confusing to readers of the financial statements.

◆ The time and costs involved in revaluing an asset portfolio can be considerable. Remember this is time and money that could be spent on growing the business.

To ensure accuracy and an impartial view an external expert will be needed at regular intervals (usually 3 or 5 years) to support the values allocated, and this will again increase the associated costs.

The mechanics of revaluation

When an asset is increased in value this requires three steps to be accurately reflected in the accounts of a company.

1. All depreciation accumulated on the asset is eliminated
2. The underlying cost of the asset is adjusted to the revised valuation
3. A revaluation reserve is created to reflect the increase in equity due to the shareholders in the hypothetical circumstances the business was shut down and the net proceeds distributed to the shareholders.

See Example 12.2

Example 12.2

Accounting for asset revaluations

On 1 January 2002 PQR Ltd purchased a property for £100,000 paying cash. Their policy is to depreciate property over a 50-year term and assume that the residual value will be zero.

On 1 January 2006 the property was professionally revalued at £138,000 and the company decided to reflect this in the financial statements. The original life-span of the asset is not considered to have changed.

Consider the impact on the financial statements for the year ended 31 December 2006.

On 1 January 2002

	Fixed assets (Property)	£100,000 (increase)
	Cash	£100,000 (decrease)

On 31 December 2002

	Depreciation expense	£2,000 (increase)
	Accumulated depreciation	£2,000 (increase)

NOTE: Remember that the accumulated depreciation is offset against the original cost of the asset in the balance sheet to leave the net book value.

On 1 January 2006

The net book value of the property will stand at £92,000 representing the original cost less four years of accumulated depreciation.

Accumulated depreciation	£8,000 (decrease)
Asset valuation	£38,000 (increase)
Revaluation reserve	£46,000 (increase)

On 31 December 2006

Depreciation expense	£3,000 (increase)
Accumulated depreciation	£3,000 (increase)

The annual depreciation expense represents the revised asset carrying value (£138,000) spread over the remaining asset life of 46 years.

As the asset value falls it is inappropriate that the revaluation reserve remains at £46,000 and so a further adjustment is made as follows.

Revaluation reserve	£1,000 (decrease)
Profit and loss reserve	£1,000 (increase)

This reserve transfer represents the revaluation reserve divided by the remaining asset life. It should be noted that this has some interesting effects on the accounts.

◆ The 'release' of the revaluation reserve has no impact on the profit and loss account and hence does not change the earnings per share.
◆ The laws of many countries place restrictions on the maximum distribution that can be made to shareholders. In the UK certain reserves shown in the equity section of the balance sheet are deemed to be non-distributable. The revaluation reserve is such a reserve, and hence it is in the interests of management to make the reserve transfer as this maximizes the distributable reserves.

Let us look at some real financial statements to see the revaluation process in action.

Box 12.1 Thorntons plc (2005) – Tangible assets note

14. Tangible assets continued

	Group 2005 £'000	Group 2004 £'000	**Company 2005 £'000**	Company 2004 £'000
Freehold and long leasehold land and buildings				
Net book value comprises:				
Freehold properties	**30,510**	31,017	**30,510**	31,005
Long leasehold properties	**188**	193	–	–
Total net book value	**30,698**	31,210	**30,510**	31,005
Cost or valuation comprises assets stated at:				
Cost	**37,973**	37,454	**37,964**	37,445
Valuation at 25 June 2005	**200**	200	–	–
Total cost or valuation	**38,173**	37,654	**37,964**	37,445

The freehold properties from which the Group trades were valued internally as at 25 June 2005 on the basis of existing use. These valuations were undertaken in accordance with the Appraisal and Valuation Manual of The Royal Institution of Chartered Surveyors in the United Kingdom by a chartered surveyor who is an employee of Thorntons PLC. These properties were last independently valued on the basis of existing use and in accordance with the Appraisal and Valuation Manual of the Royal Institution of Chartered Surveyors in the United Kingdom by Reid Rose Gregory in October 2003. The valuations are not significantly different from those recognised in the financial statements and the Directors consider that no changes in the carrying values are required.

If stated under historical cost principles, the comparable amounts for the total of freehold and long leasehold land and buildings would be:

	Group **2005** **£'000**	Group 2004 £'000	**Company** **2005** **£'000**	Company 2004 £'000
Cost	**37,992**	37,473	**37,964**	37,445
Accumulated depreciation	**(7,477)**	(6,449)	**(7,454)**	(6,440)
Net book value	**30,515**	31,024	**30,510**	31,005

Plant and machinery with a cost of £6,242,000 (2004: £2,635,000) has not been depreciated during the year as it has not been fully commissioned.

This represents the annual depreciation charge including the additional depreciation arising from the upward revaluation of the underlying assets

4. Operating profit	2005 £'000	2004 £'000
Operating profit is stated after charging/(crediting):		
Depreciation of owned tangible fixed assets	7,634	7,575
Depreciation of tangible fixed assets held under finance lease	4,081	3,624
Operating lease rentals – land and buildings	18,863	19,126
– other	810	994
Hire of plant and machinery	104	107
Rents payable in relation to store turnover	471	469
Auditors' remuneration – parent company	80	58
– audit-related regulatory reporting	25	–
– subsidiaries	2	2
Corporation tax fees paid to auditors	115	98
Other non-audit fees paid to auditors	195	55
Net charge to onerous lease and dilapidation provisions	309	324
Amortisation of government grant	(16)	(8)
Loss on disposal of fixed assets (excluding properties)	10	17

Illustration 12.2 Thorntons plc (2005) – Operating profit note

The basis of the depreciation charge and the underlying treatment of the tangible assets can be found in the accounting policy note.

Box 12.2   Thorntons plc (2005) – Accounting policy extract

Tangible fixed assets and depreciation

Tangible fixed assets are stated at cost or valuation less accumulated depreciation. Cost comprises the purchase price of tangible fixed assets together with any incidental costs of acquisition. Specific internal employee costs incurred in implementing capital projects of the Group are capitalised within fixed assets in the same category as the project.

Valuations of freehold properties, from which the Group trades, are undertaken annually by a chartered surveyor who is an employee of Thorntons PLC. Every third year, the valuations are provided by an external firm of chartered surveyors. These valuations are compared with those already recognised in the financial statements and if not significantly different, then no changes to the carrying values are made.

All tangible assets, other than land and assets in the course of construction, are depreciated to write off the assets over their remaining useful lives by equal annual instalments, as follows:

In equal annual instalments:

Freehold premises	50 years
Short leasehold land and buildings	Period of the lease
Retail fixtures and fittings	5 years
Retail equipment	4 to 5 years
Retail store improvements	10 years
Computer software	3 to 5 years
Other equipment and vehicles	3 to 7 years
Manufacturing plant and machinery	12 to 15 years

The need for an impairment write-down is assessed by comparison of the carrying value of the asset against the higher of its net realisable value or its value in use.

24. Reserves

Group	Share premium account £'000	Revaluation reserves £'000	Profit and loss account £'000
At 26 June 2004 as previously reported	12,483	186	24,384
Investment in own shares	—	—	(2,310)
At 26 June 2004 as restated	12,483	186	22,074
New shares issues	45	—	—
Movement in investment in own shares	—	—	161
Transfer between reserves	—	(3)	3
Retained profit for the period	—	—	1,110
At 25 June 2005	**12,528**	**183**	**23,348**

This is the transfer from the non-distributable revaluation reserve to the profit and loss reserve

Illustration 12.3 Thorntons plc (2005) – Reserves note extract

Historic cost vs. current cost

The concept of asset revaluation draws us to one of the longest and most contentious arguments in the world of accounting. Is it better to use historic assets values (i.e. those that applied at the date of acquisition) or current market values?

Advantages of using historic cost

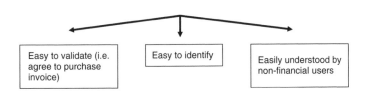

Easy to validate (i.e. agree to purchase invoice)

Easy to identify

Easily understood by non-financial users

Disadvantages of using historic cost

Inflation is a familiar concept that often makes the headlines on television or is a point of conversation as people discuss the cost of living, and it is the fact that historic cost accounting ignores inflation that undermines its credibility as a method for preparing financial information.

1. Current revenues are not matched to current costs leading to an overstatement of profits in real terms.

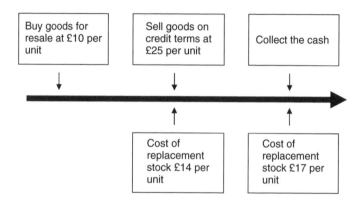

Using historic cost accounting a profit of £15 will be recorded on each unit sold, but at the date of sale £14 will be needed to replace the stock sold. If the company wants to continue trading without recourse to additional funding the real terms profit is £11. It should be noted that in reality this is a simplification as the £14 is not collected on the date of sale, and hence cash has not flowed into the business – this shows the difficulties faced by management when trying to estimate the timing of receipts and balancing this with cash flows from trading and financing to enable the replacement of goods sold.

The problems are further compounded when consideration is given to the cost of replacement stock on the date cash is received from customers as prices have risen again.

These factors will also influence the dividend policy of a business as to pay large dividends could be reckless in times of strong positive inflation as they may undermine the ability of the business to buy replacement stock.

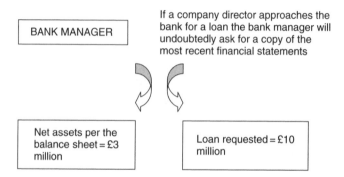

The chances of receiving a loan of this size are slim as the bank will be looking to secure the borrowing against the assets of the business which appear totally inadequate. However, what if several of the assets are properties purchased 30 years previously, and which now have a depreciated historic cost carrying value of £50,000. These are located on prestigious sites and now have a current market value of £27 million making the loan look less of a risky proposition to the provider of finance.

3. Trend analysis – if historic cost accounting distorts both profits and asset values this makes ratio comparison over time a risky business.

4. Do not put money under the mattress!
    There is a common perception of elderly relatives putting all their money under the mattress for safe-keeping as they do not trust the bank. Unfortunately in times of positive inflation the purchasing power of this monetary asset is dwindling. In a similar way the effect of price changes on fixed monetary items is not recognized by historic cost accounts.

Based on the weight of evidence above you might believe that every company would be trying to move towards current cost accounting, but in practice this is not the case. It is primarily the accounting profession who would like to see such a progression, but it is fraught with difficulties notably reaching a consensus on what constitutes the fair value of the wide and diverse range of assets seen in modern business.

Impairment – taking bad news on the chin

There are occasions when the value of an asset will fall dramatically over a short period, and prudence dictates that this must be recognized so that profits and asset value are not overstated.

Picture the assets within a typical business – how could such an impairment of value occur?

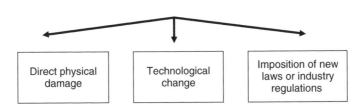

Impairments can often be for large amounts and hence their accounting treatment can be key to an understanding of the accounts.

Basic rule

> Asset value (decreases)
> Expense (increases)

The expense will usually be disclosed separately either on the face of the profit and loss account or in the notes. To obtain a clear picture regarding the future performance of the business this expense should be excluded from your analysis due to its one-off nature.

Impairment of revalued assets

> Asset value (decreases)
> Revaluation reserve (decreases)

If the revaluation reserve is fully utilized then any excess impairment will be expensed.

At this stage your newly primed analytical mind is probably firing questions into your consciousness. Let us consider some of the queries you may have.

Query 1: *When an asset is impaired how is the new carrying value determined?*

There is rarely an exact science to the valuation of an asset as the ultimate test lies in the price a willing purchaser is prepared to pay. This is a dilemma as the business may have no intention of disposing of the asset. The accounting guidance given below has considerable flex, and a management team could take advantage of this when calculating the size of the impairment.

An impairment has occurred if:

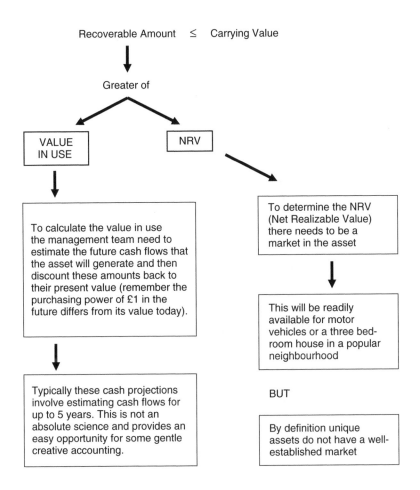

Recoverable Amount ≤ Carrying Value

Greater of

VALUE
IN USE

NRV

To calculate the value in use
the management team need to
estimate the future cash flows that
the asset will generate and then
discount these amounts back to
their present value (remember the
purchasing power of £1 in the
future differs from its value today).

To determine the NRV
(Net Realizable Value)
there needs to be a
market in the asset

This will be readily
available for motor
vehicles or a three bed-
room house in a popular
neighbourhood

Typically these cash projections
involve estimating cash flows for
up to 5 years. This is not an
absolute science and provides an
easy opportunity for some gentle
creative accounting.

BUT

By definition unique
assets do not have a well-
established market

Query 2: *How will management know if an impairment has occurred?*

Sometimes the evidence of an impairment is obvious such as direct physical damage, but other impairments are less obvious and there is an onus on management to have a system of review to ensure that indicators are spotted and addressed.

If during you analysis of the figures you have an opportunity to discuss the derivation of the numbers then ask about the indicators they have identified, but also consider potential indicators based on your own commercial awareness and enquire why they have not had the impact you might have expected.

> Example: The increasing emphasis on environmental issues and the reduction in harmful emissions means that old equipment should be reviewed for impairment attributable to non-compliance with harsher environmental rules and regulations.

Query 3: *Is it reasonable to expect the managers of a large and widely distributed company to regularly inspect every asset for signs of impairment?*

The answer to this question is obviously 'no', but what represents a reasonable compromise between prudent management and the expenditure of disproportionate resources that could be better exercised maximizing shareholder wealth?

It is usual for assets to be aggregated together. Under UK GAAP these groupings are known as 'Income Generating Units' whereas under international GAAP they called 'Cash Generating Units'. Although there is some accounting guidance to determine the boundaries of each unit this is another inexact science.

> Example (a simple scenario): A company operating three restaurants would view each as a separate unit. It is easy to identify the costs and revenues of each restaurant.

> Example (a tougher scenario): A company has four divisions which exchange assets and utilize a common administration and marketing centre. In this situation it would be difficult to identify boundaries between potential units.

In summary the decision to impair an asset can have a dramatic impact on financial information not only in the year of the decision but thereafter.

Asset turnover	Increase	
Debt/equity ratio	Increase	Year of
Current profit margin: year of impairment	Decrease	impairment
Future ROE: years following impairment	Increase	

Capitalization vs. expensing

You will remember that every accounting transaction has two sides, and it is this fundamental idea that explains why an unscrupulous manager may look to exploit the capitalization/expensing decision.

Example 12.3

Capitalization vs. expensing

XYZ Ltd pays £50,000 to refurbish its head office, and some of the directors have asked to see the impact on the financial statements of expensing and capitalizing this cost.

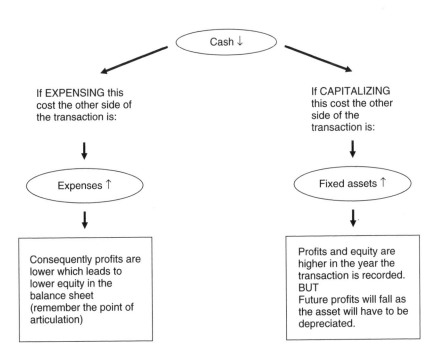

This decision should not be a free choice but driven by the nature of the cost and a decision regarding the existence of future benefits, but this is not always easy. Consider what the £50,000 has been used to buy:

◆ Redecoration – undoubtedly an expense as future benefit cannot be directly attributed to this cost. Although an inventive manager may claim that it results in more customers being drawn to the premises.

◆ Construction of small retail outlet within the building – Capitalization seems appropriate as the retail outlet should either generate additional sales or if let to a third party will produce a new revenue stream in the form of rental income.

The impact of the capitalization decision on the key financial ratios derived from the financial statements can be dramatic. The following table considers the consequences in the year the transaction occurs.

	Variable	Expensing	Capitalizing
1	Profits	Lower	Higher
2	Shareholders' equity	Lower	Higher
3	Cash flow	Same	Same
4	Asset turnover	Higher	Lower
5	Current ratio	Same	Same
6	Debt-to-equity	Higher	Lower
7	Return on equity	Lower	Higher

1. Expensing all the cost directly impacts profits.
2. If profits are reduced there is less to transfer to reserves at the period end and as a consequence equity is lower compared to capitalization.

3. Irrespective of the accounting method used the cash has been spent and so cash flows are identical.
4. Asset turnover decreases when costs are capitalized as they are now included within fixed assets on the balance sheet. Turnover (i.e. sales) has not changed as a consequence of this accounting decision.
5. The current ratio compares current assets with current liabilities and so is unaffected as capitalization increases fixed assets only.
6. Capitalization leads to increased equity whilst long-term debt is unaffected, and hence gearing improves (i.e. it gets lower).
7. Capitalization also improves return on equity although this is the most subtle of the consequences because both profits and equity have increased! However for most companies equity will be a larger number than profit and so in proportionate terms will change by less.

Example 12.4

Impact of proportionate changes on the return on equity

If the profit of XYZ Ltd had been £175,000 and the equity £500,000

◆ ROCE before transaction $= \dfrac{175,000}{500,000} = 35\%$

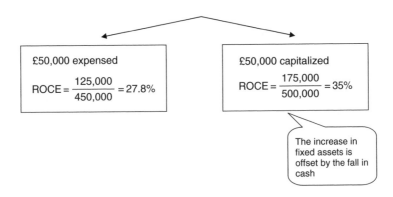

Do not forget that if the decision is taken to capitalize costs this will have a detrimental impact on future profits as the asset created in the balance sheet is depreciated. As a reviewer you would try to identify commercial issues that may drive management to make borderline decisions. In most cases the desire will be to improve profits now as this could improve remuneration, enhance the share price and reputation of the management team who may have moved on before the downsides of their decision become reality.

The costs of financing construction

When buying a completed property the price paid is designed to cover all the costs of the construction company and provide a modest profit. The aforementioned costs will include the cost of finance (i.e. interest).

Consequently if a company decides to construct a property there is a consistent logic that they should be permitted to capitalize the costs of borrowing.

In the UK and Europe there are accounting rules which determine if capitalization is appropriate, but if these conditions are met the final decision is one of choice for the management team. This differs from the USA were capitalization is mandatory if the amounts are material to an understanding of the financial statements. Again we need to be aware of these disparities if a meaningful comparison is to be made.

The things every manager must know

1. When a fixed asset is initially recorded the 'cost' includes all direct costs associated with its acquisition and necessary for bringing it into normal use.
2. Depreciation is a mechanism by which cost is matched to the periods which benefit from the use of the asset.
3. Depreciation can be implemented using straight line or accelerated methodologies, and in all cases involves extensive use of estimation (e.g. useful economic life).
4. Land is not depreciated.
5. Under UK and international GAAP the upward revaluation of fixed assets is allowed but not required.
6. Revaluation enhances asset values in the balance sheet but reduces profits through increased depreciation, and thereby has a dramatic impact on key ratios such as return on capital employed.
7. Assets should not be held in the balance at amounts in excess of their recoverable amount. Any impairment should be recognized

against profits for the year unless the asset has previously been revalued upwards creating a revaluation reserve.

8. The decision to capitalize or expense has been the basis for several high profile corporate frauds – the temptation being to carry 'costs' as an asset in the balance sheet on the pretence that future benefits will accrue against which they can be offset.

Hidden Value – Intangible Assets

What constitutes an intangible asset?

When one company makes an acquisition of another the price paid will not be equal to the value of the net assets as shown by the balance sheet. This should come as no surprise as we have already seen that the carrying value of many assets shown in the balance sheet does not equal their market value, but this is not the sole explanation for the disparity. If the company acquired has been established for a long period it will have built up a reputation, its staff will have unique expertise and customer loyalty will have been generated; all of these add value to the business and will be reflected in the acquisition price.

The additional premium paid by the acquirer for assets that lack physical substance is often in excess of that paid for the assets that can be seen and touched. The intangible asset we have described is more formally known as goodwill, but there are numerous other intangible assets:

◆ Royalties
◆ Franchises
◆ Intellectual property
◆ Development costs
◆ Brands
◆ Customer lists.

The nature of many intangibles makes them difficult to identify and value, but for the potential analyst of financial data this is just the start of their dilemma. Some intangibles appear on the balance sheet as an asset but others do not, and to make matters more confusing the major accounting regimes (e.g. UK GAAP, International GAAP, etc.) have differing approaches.

To help understand the key issues for a reviewer we will examine three key categories.

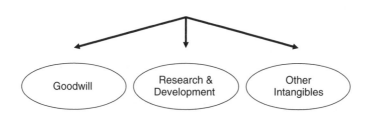

Goodwill

Observed from a technical perspective, an asset (any asset) is a resource controlled by an entity as a result of a past event and from which future benefits are expected to flow. Intangible assets fall beneath this umbrella but have the additional characteristics that they are non-monetary and lack physical substance.

Goodwill has a further unique feature which is that unlike all other assets it is not identifiable and as such is recognized by 'default' as the difference between the fair value paid to acquire a business and the fair value of the identifiable net assets acquired.

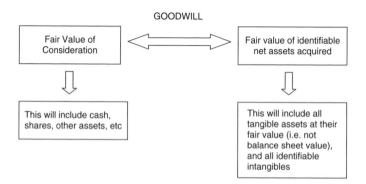

It is important to note that goodwill can only be recognized on a company balance sheet when it has been acquired.

> INTERNALLY GENERATED GOODWILL CAN NEVER BE RECOGNIZED

This is logical as until it is purchased the value of goodwill cannot be known as it will be unique to that business.

Purchased goodwill will often be separately disclosed from other intangible assets on the face of the balance sheet (see Illustration 13.1), but it is always worth checking the intangible note for a full understanding (see Illustration 13.1).

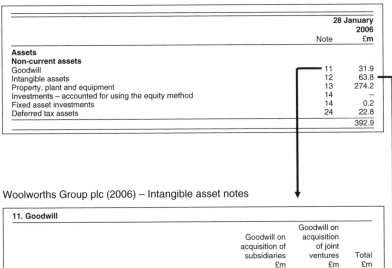

	Note	28 January 2006 £m
Assets		
Non-current assets		
Goodwill	11	31.9
Intangible assets	12	63.8
Property, plant and equipment	13	274.2
Investments – accounted for using the equity method	14	–
Fixed asset investments	14	0.2
Deferred tax assets	24	22.8
		392.9

Woolworths Group plc (2006) – Intangible asset notes

11. Goodwill

	Goodwill on acquisition of subsidiaries £m	Goodwill on acquisition of joint ventures £m	Total £m
Cost			
At 30 January 2005	31.2	38.4	69.6
Additions	–	0.1	0.1
At 28 January 2006	31.2	38.5	69.7
Impairment			
At 30 January 2005 and at 28 January 2006	(31.2)	(6.6)	(37.8)
Net book amount			
At 28 January 2006	–	31.9	31.9

12. Intangible Assets

	Brands £m	Underlying rights £m	Purchased copyrights and licences £m	Software £m	Total intangible assets £m
Cost					
At 30 January 2005	15.0	30.1	2.6	90.6	138.3
Additions	–	–	1.5	9.1	10.6
At 28 January 2006	15.0	30.1	4.1	99.7	148.9
Amortisation					
At 30 January 2005	(3.0)	(1.0)	(0.6)	(65.2)	(69.8)
Change for the year	(0.7)	(3.0)	(1.6)	(10.0)	(15.3)
At 28 January 2006	(3.7)	(4.0)	(2.2)	(75.2)	(85.1)
Net book amount					
At 28 January 2006	11.3	26.1	1.9	24.5	63.8

Illustration 13.1 Woolworths Group plc (2006) – Balance sheet extract

You will already understand why goodwill is a major concern to any analyst of financial statements as its initial carrying value is dependent upon the accurate identification of the other assets acquired. This partially explains the emphasis placed upon a due diligence review of the target company by external professionals prior to an acquisition.

However, the task of the reviewer is made more challenging by the subsequent accounting treatment of goodwill as this is dependent upon which GAAP is used in the preparation of the financial statements.

Under UK GAAP the core principle focuses on the amortization of goodwill. Do not be concerned by the term 'amortization' as it is the equivalent to depreciation for tangible assets.

UK GAAP

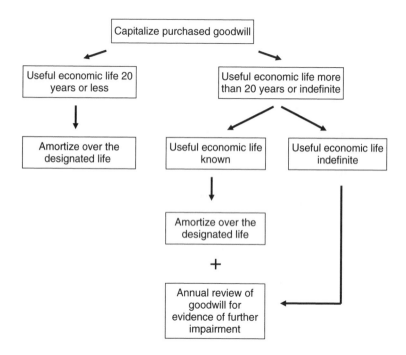

International GAAP

There is no amortization of goodwill which is replaced by an annual impairment review.

The international approach can create additional volatility in the reported performance of the business, compared to a steady annual amortization charge. This is usually addressed by stripping both depreciation and amortization from the figures together with tax and interest to present the true operational performance of the business.

The figure generated is known as EBITDA (earnings before interest, taxation, depreciation and amortization).

Negative goodwill

On rare occasions the consideration given will be less than the value of the net assets acquired giving rise to negative goodwill.

Under UK GAAP this is shown on the balance sheet immediately below positive goodwill on other acquisitions, but under international GAAP it is immediately taken to the profit and loss account. This has the effect of inflating the profits for that period, and would normally be excluded when reviewing the true performance of the business.

Research and development

For some business sectors such as computing and pharmaceuticals expenditure on research and development is a predeterminant to corporate survival, and consequently the figures involved are some of the most material within the financial statements.

The treatment of research costs is straightforward if you recall one of the key features in defining an asset, namely that it will generate future benefits. Although this is the hope of the researcher it is not possible to determine if their embryonic studies will result in a successful product being brought to market.

> ALL EXPENDITURE ON RESEARCH MUST BE EXPENSED AS INCURRED

This will reduce profits and have a detrimental impact on key indicators such as earnings per share and return on equity in the current period. This means great care must be taken when reviewing the figures, as disappointing results do not necessarily imply the company is failing, but simply that it is investing for the future. For large research-orientated companies these fluctuations may be masked by having numerous products at differing stages of their life cycle, but problems can arise when a much-vaunted product fails at the final trial, leaving a hole in future revenues that had not been anticipated.

The dividing line between when research to identify a product ends and development of an identified product begins is not always clear. Criteria used by the accounting profession include:

◆ Technical feasibility of completing development, thereby bringing the product to a saleable state.
◆ The intention exists to complete the asset so that it is ready for use or sale.
◆ Ability to use or sell the resultant asset.
◆ Ability to demonstrate the existence of a market.
◆ Consideration to determine if adequate technical and financial resources exist to complete the development.
◆ The expenditure incurred can be reliably identified.

These benchmarks look commendable but practical implementation is often difficult. The ability to demonstrate the existence of a market for the product usually involves market research but there is no guarantee that customers will eventually make a purchase.

Companies will also fine tune these criteria to ensure a sensible consistency with accepted best practice within their sector (Box 13.1).

Box 13.1 Box 13.1 GlaxoSmithKline plc (2005) – Accounting policy extract

Research and development

Research and development expenditure is charged to the income statement in the period in which it is incurred. Development expenditure is capitalised when the criteria for recognising an asset are met, usually when a regulatory filing has been made in a major market and approval is considered highly probable. Property, plant and equipment used for research and development is depreciated in accordance with the Group's policy.

If sufficient evidence exists that the criteria described have been met then it is normal for the costs to be capitalized and held as an intangible asset on the balance sheet. This asset will not be amortized, but will be released against profits when commercial use or sales begin. The pattern of release will be linked to projections about the period of future benefit and the pattern of sales; clearly this creates some uncertainty for the reviewer as they will rarely have access to the basis of such information.

It should be noted that when development recognition criteria have been met international GAAP requires mandatory capitalization whereas UK GAAP stills allows the choice of immediate expensing if preferred. If the company you are reviewing complies with US accounting rules the dilemma is eliminated as they require expensing of both research and development costs.

Other intangibles

There are many intangibles that could be brought onto the balance sheet thereby enhancing net assets, but the question you should ask is whether such treatment is appropriate. This is particularly true of brands which many companies started to reflect on their balance sheets in the 1980s and 1990s, claiming that this was vital to more fully reflect shareholder value and to allow management to be called to account if values fell. It also begs the question that if a brand is capitalized should it then be amortized; some famous brands continue to generate customer loyalty more than 100 years after they were launched.

When reviewing the financial statements of a company to determine the appropriateness of including designated intangible assets on its balance sheet, key questions to ask include the following.

Question 1

Is the potential asset capable of reliable measurement and will it generate probable future economic benefits?

It is difficult to justify the capitalization of advertising expenditure – proving that a future sale was generated specifically from the adverts rather than other commercial factors will be difficult.

Question 2

Is the asset identifiable?

This can be sub-divided into:

It is sufficient if one of these criteria is met, but usually it is both

1. Is it separable (i.e. could it be sold separately)?
2. Does it arise from contractual or legal rights?

A purchased patent or copyright meets both criteria

Rights that allow a tangible asset to be used such as distribution rights are not separable but do convey a legal right, and would be deemed to be identifiable.

Question 3

Does the entity control the asset?

Such control would normally arise from the contractual or legal rights previously described, but this is not always the case.

A secret recipe known to only a few individuals would be effectively controlled by them

These tests are derived from international accounting standards but serve as a useful litmus test under any circumstances. Review Exercise 13.1 to practise your new skills.

Exercise 13.1

Recognition of intangible assets

For each of the following scenarios consider if it is appropriate based on the information available to recognize an intangible asset in the balance sheet.

1. First team players for a professional football club
2. A North Sea fishing quota

3. Customer loyalty
4. Subsequent expenditure on an intangible asset already recognized in the balance sheet.

Make sure you have considered your answer before referring to the solutions below. Intangible assets are one of the most challenging areas you will encounter in your review of financial information, and it is important that you have practised using the ground rules.

Solutions

Scenario 1

It is never appropriate to put people on the balance sheet as an employee always has the right to resign, and hence can never be controlled by the company. If you review the financial statements of a football club it would be easy to believe that they have transgressed

		Group	
		30 June 2005	30 June 2004
	Note	£'000	£'000
Fixed assets			
Intangible assets	12	31,348	25,053
Tangible assets	13	49,105	48,219
Investments	14	–	–
		80,453	73,272

12. Intangible fixed assets Group	£000
Cost of registrations	
At 1 July 2004	43,463
Additions	24,605
Disposals	(19,511)
At 30 June 2005	48,557
Amortisation and impairment of registrations	
At 1 July 2004	18,410
Charged in year – amortisation	12,741
Disposals	(13,942)
At 30 June 2005	17,209
Net book value of registrations	
At 30 June 2005	31,348
At 30 June 2004	25,053

Figure 13.2 Tottenham Hotspur plc (2005) – Extracts from the balance sheet and notes

this rule, but in reality they do not include their players as assets on the balance but do record the player registrations (Figure 13.2).

The registrations of players who have been developed through the youth scheme of the club cannot be included as an intangible asset as they have never been purchased. As each player is unique the value of their registration cannot be reliably measured unless an exchange transaction has taken place at arms length in the open market.

Scenario 2

Although this sounds unusual to anyone not operating in this industrial sector, such a quota can be recognized in the balance sheet as it is identifiable, can be reliably measured (i.e. the price paid) and is expected to give future benefits in the form of fish catches.

NOTE: With increasing restrictions being implemented to preserve dwindling fish stocks you may want to enquire if this asset is likely to suffer an impairment to its value.

Scenario 3

Customer loyalty or any similar form of customer relationship does not meet the criteria for capitalization as an intangible asset as the value cannot be reliably measured. However, if the contact details of customers could be sold to another interested party to facilitate marketing by the latter the amount received could be considered as an asset.

Scenario 4

Subsequent expenditure on an intangible asset is usually to maintain the asset rather than improve it and as such does not provide future benefits. In the majority of instances such expenditure will be expensed.

In summary if an intangible has been purchased separately or as part of a bigger acquisition there is a strong probability that it should be recognized as a balance-sheet asset. Internally generated assets are rarely recognized with the exception of development costs as previously described, although UK GAAP allows recognition if there is a readily ascertainable market value as might be the case with a franchise.

If recognized these assets should be amortized over their useful economic life. This time span is easily identified for patents and royalty agreements, but involves considerable discretion for other assets allowing further opportunities for creative accounting.

The things every manager must know

1. Goodwill is the residual difference between the fair value of consideration given to purchase a business and the fair value of the identifiable net assets acquired.
2. Under international accounting rules goodwill is reviewed annually for impairment but there is no regular amortization expense. This contrasts with UK GAAP where amortization is the favoured method.
3. Internally generated goodwill should never be recognized as an asset.
4. Research costs are always expensed, but development costs will be capitalized if certain criteria such as technical feasibility are met. Under UK GAAP such capitalization remains an option but is likely to be taken up by management looking to strengthen the balance sheet.
5. Other intangibles should only be recognized if they are
   - Identifiable
   - Controlled
   - Capable of reliable measurement
   - Give rise to future economic benefits.

14

An Introduction to
Investments

Parent company vs. group

If you were to pick up the glossy annual financial statements for a large listed company and turn to the balance sheet the chances are that you will see something similar to that in Box 14.1.

Box 14.1 Thorntons plc (2005) Balance sheet

	Notes	**Group** As at **25 June 2005** £'000	Group As at 26 June 2004 (as restated) £'000	**Company** As at **25 June 2005** £'000	Company As at 26 June 2004 (as restated) £'000
Fixed assets					
Tangible assets	14	**79,544**	80,329	**79,330**	80,102
Investment in subsidiaries	15	–	–	**18**	18
		79,544	80,329	**79,348**	80,120
Current assets					
Stocks	16	**17,958**	18,912	**17,947**	18,904
Debtors	17	**13,592**	12,818	**21,888**	14,108
Cash at bank and in hand		**874**	1,599	**580**	848
		32,424	33,329	**40,415**	33,860
Creditors: amounts falling due within one year	18	**(52,902)**	(48,788)	**(62,789)**	(50,950)
Net current liabilities		**(20,478)**	(15,459)	**(22,374)**	(17,090)
Total assets less current liabilities		**59,066**	64,870	**56,974**	63,030
Creditors: amounts falling due after one year	19	**(7,247)**	(14,568)	**(7,247)**	(14,568)
Provisions for liabilities and charges	22	**(9,091)**	(8,896)	**(8,996)**	(8,789)
Net assets		**42,728**	41,406	**40,731**	39,673
Capital and reserves					
Share capital	23	**6,669**	6,663	**6,669**	6,663
Share premium	24	**12,528**	12,483	**12,528**	12,483
Revaluation reserves	24	**183**	186	–	–
Profit and loss account	24	**23,348**	22,074	**21,534**	20,527
Equity shareholders' funds		**42,728**	41,406	**40,731**	39,673

There appears to be two balance sheets for each year!

This is because the company has investments in the share capital of others and these companies are aggregated to form the group accounts, also known as the consolidated financial statements. We will take a closer look at some of the key processes and analytical consequences of group accounts in a later chapter, but for the moment let us concentrate on the balance sheet of the parent company only.

What constitutes an investment?

When a company purchases shares in another company it is said to have made an investment in that company, and will benefit from dividend payments just like any other shareholder.

In the individual balance sheet of the parent company this investment is recorded at cost, and on the presumption that it is intended to hold the shares for the long term these will be held within the fixed-assets section of the balance sheet. They are not subject to depreciation or amortization, but as with any asset should be reviewed regularly to ensure that the value has not been impaired.

Tracking the investments line back into the notes can provide a useful insight into the nature of the investments made by the company (Figure 14.1).

In Figure 14.1 it can be seen that the parent company owns all of the share capital of the investments, but this will not always be the case and will be crucial if you are to understand the methods used to prepare group financial statements, which is covered in a later chapter.

The major categories of investment include:

Subsidiary   The operating and financial decisions of this company are controlled by the parent. In most circumstances this involves a shareholding in excess of 50 per cent.

Associate   The operating and financial decisions of an associate are influenced by the parent company but it does not have outright control. Typically this involves a shareholding between 20 per cent and 50 per cent.

	Notes	2006 £m
FIXED ASSETS		
Investments	7	**1,738**
CURRENT ASSETS		
Debtors	8	622
Investments		114
Cash at bank and in hand		172
		908
Creditors: amounts falling due within one year	9	(1,692)
NET CURRENT LIABILITIES		**(784)**
NET ASSETS BEFORE NET PENSION LIABILITIES		**954**
Net pension liabilities	3	(65)
NET ASSETS		**889**
CAPITAL AND RESERVES		
Called up share capital	10	34
Share premium account	11	14
Capital redemption reserve	11	3
Profit and loss account reserve	11	838
EQUITY SHAREHOLDERS' FUNDS		**889**

7. Fixed asset investments

	Shares in group undertakings £m
Cost	
At 2 October 2005 and 30 September 2006	**1,745**
Provision	
At 2 October 2005	6
Provided during year	1
At 30 September 2006	**7**
Net book value	
At 30 September 2006	**1,738**
At 1 October 2005	1,739

Mitchells & Butlers plc is the beneficial owner of all of the equity share captial, either itself or through subsidiary undertakings, of the following prinicipal operating comparities:

Name of subsidiary	Country of incorporation	Country of operation	Nature of business
Mitchells & Butlers Retail Ltd	England and Wales	United Kingdom	Leisure retailing
Mitchells & Butlers Retail (No 2) Ltd	England and Wales	United Kingdom	Leisure retailing
Mitchells & Butlers (Property) Ltd	England and Wales	United Kingdom	Property management
Mitchells & Butlers Leisure Retail Ltd	England and Wales	United Kingdom	Service company
Mitchells & Butlers Finance plc	England and Wales	United Kingdom	Finance company
Mitchells & Butlers Germany GmbH*	Germany	Germany	Leisure retailing
Standard Commercial Property Developments Ltd*	England and Wales	United Kingdom	Property development

*Shares held directly by Mitchells & Butlers plc

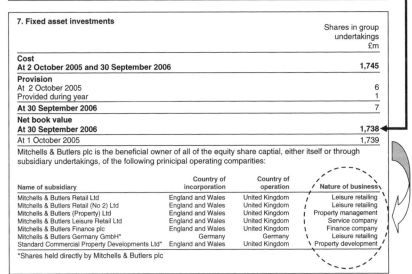

Figure 14.1 Mitchells & Butlers plc (2006) – Parent company balance sheet extract and investments note

A jointly controlled entity (a form of joint venture)	As the name implies the parent company has shared control with one or more other venturers.
Trade Investment	The parent company has neither control nor influence over such an investment and typically this involves a shareholding of less than 20 per cent.

The things every manager must know

1. In the financial statements of the parent company an investment in the shares of another company will be shown at cost unless subsequently impaired.
2. There are several categories of investment designated by the level of control or influence that the parent company can exercise over their operating and financial decisions.

Leasing and the Concept of Commercial Substance Prevailing over Legal form

Why choose to lease an asset?

There was a time when leasing an asset was seen as the 'poor mans' option' for those who could not afford to buy an asset outright, but today it is seen as a key element of company finance for many organizations. Potential advantages of leasing an asset include:

1. It reduces cash flow volatility as there are regular payments instead of a single lump sum, and also preserves other credit lines which can be used for investment in working capital.
2. It allows access to assets that a business could not afford to buy outright, and, in many instances, allows 100 per cent finance with no security deposits.
3. Depending on the type of lease agreement it is a method of off balance sheet finance which can improve the apparent financial performance and position of the company.
4. Leasing allows a balance to be reached between usage and cost which is particularly useful when the asset is required for substantially less than its useful economic life.
5. Many lease agreements allow an element of flexibility whereby at the end of the primary term the asset can be returned, purchased or the term of the lease extended.

The concept of commercial substance prevailing over legal form

To understand the accounting implications of lease agreements for the financial statements, it is essential to understand the concept of commercial substance prevailing over legal form.

There is a famous phrase that states 'laws are to be broken', and whilst this is not a strategy that would normally be a feature of good corporate governance this is one occasion when these words hold an element of truth. It is important to remember that financial statements are designed to fulfil a range of purposes such as assisting a potential investor in their decision-making, and we must consider what they would prefer to be shown.

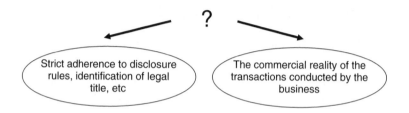

There is little doubt that they would like to know what is really happening, and hence in those circumstances when legal form and commercial substance conflict it is the latter that should prevail.

Differentiating operating and finance leases

We will consider the two types of lease from the perspective of the lessee as this is the most relevant for the majority of instances when we will be reviewing financial information.

OPERATING LEASES		FINANCE LEASES
Legal title rests with the lessor	Legal title to the asset	Legal title rests with the lessor
Operating leases are consistent with a short-term rental, and, in substance, ownership of the asset still lies with the lessor	Commercial substance	The majority of the risks and rewards of ownership have passed to the lessee who, in substance, treats the asset as if they own it

The asset should be recorded in the balance sheet of the lessor

The asset should be shown on the balance sheet of the lessee in spite of the fact that they do not legally own it

This is an example of off balance sheet finance (see later sections)

The transfer of risks and rewards

There are no hard and fast rules to determine when the risks and rewards of ownership have to be transferred from the lessor to the lessee (except under US GAAP where the rules are more prescriptive). Typical considerations would be:

◆ Who maintains and insures the asset?
◆ Who bears the cost of idle time?
◆ Who uses the asset for the majority of its useful economic life?

In the majority of cases the intention of the lease contract will make this a straightforward decision, but there will also be some borderline cases. In these circumstances a more technical question is asked, namely:

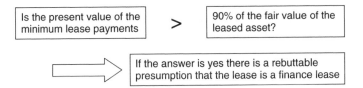

Accounting consequences of the lease decision

If a lease is designated as an operating lease the accounting consequences are straightforward.

$$\text{Annual Lease Expense} = \frac{\textit{Total Lease Payments}}{\textit{Lease Term}}$$

As shown by Example 15.1 this does not necessarily mean that the cash payments made in a period will be equal to the lease rental

Example 15.1

Operating lease accounting

A manufacturing company enters into a 3-year operating lease for plant and machinery. The lease terms require an upfront payment of £3,000 followed by further payments of £4,000 at the end of each period.

$$\text{Annual Lease Expense} = \frac{£3000 + (3 \times £4000)}{3 \text{ Years}} = £5,000$$

In year 1 the company paid £7,000 in cash effectively prepaying £2,000 relating to later periods and this will be shown in the balance sheet as a prepayment.

To identify the operating lease expense for the period reference will need to be made to the financial statement notes.

Box 15.1 Laura Ashley Holdings plc (2006) – Profit from operations note

3   profit from operations is stated after charging/(crediting):

	2006 £m	2005 £m
Depreciation on property, plant and equipment (note 11)	6.1	6.3
Exchange gains	(0.3)	(0.7)
Profit on disposal of property, plant and equipment	(0.3)	(1.0)
Operating lease and hire charges of:		
Property	19.4	22.4
Others	2.5	2.7
Auditors' remuneration	0.2	0.3
Cost of inventories recognised as an expense	105.5	122.6
Including: Reversal of provision for inventories obsolescence	(0.6)	–
Provision for inventories obsolescence	–	0.3

Finance lease accounting is more complex as substance must prevail over legal form, and consequently the lessee will include the leased asset on its own balance sheet.

Hence on day 1 of the lease agreement the lessee will make the following entries to the accounting records.

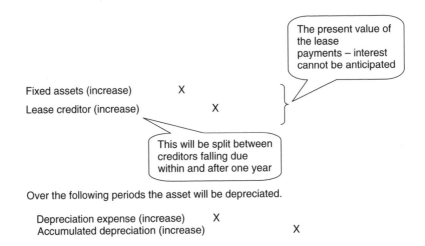

Over the following periods the asset will be depreciated.

Depreciation expense (increase)	X	
Accumulated depreciation (increase)		X

In the fixed asset note companies will either show assets held under finance leases as a separate section or will amalgamate leased assets with those they own and then give additional information at the foot of the note to assist the reader in identifying leased assets. Further information on the accumulated depreciation and depreciation expense can also be found within this note.

Box 15.2 Laura Ashley Holdings plc (2006) – Fixed asset note

11 property, plant and equipment

Group	land and buildings freehold £m	short leases £m	plant, machinery and vehicles £m	fixtures, fittings and equipment £m	paid on account and under Construction £m	total £m
Cost						
At 30 January 2005	21.6	12.0	8.3	48.9	0.8	91.6
Additions	0.4	1.6	–	1.5	–	3.5
Disposals	–	(2.8)	–	(1.8)	–	(4.6)
At 28 January 2006	22.0	10.6	8.3	48.6	0.8	90.5
Depreciation						
At 30 January 2005	8.4	4.3	8.0	39.0	–	59.7
Change for the year	0.3	1.0	0.1	4.7	–	6.1
Disposals	–	(2.5)	–	(1.9)	–	(4.4)
At 28 January 2006	8.7	2.8	8.1	41.8	–	61.4
Net book value						
At 28 January 2006	13.3	8.0	0.2	6.8	0.8	29.1
At 29 January 2005	13.2	7.7	0.3	9.9	0.8	31.9

The net book value of property, plant and equipment includes an amount of £0.8 million (2005: £1.8 million) in respect of assets held under finance leases and hire purchase contracts. The depreciation of these assets in the year amounted to £1.0 million (2005: £1.4 million).

Each lease payment made will comprise of two elements – one portion representing the repayment of outstanding capital and the other portion representing interest. As with a normal repayment mortgage with which many of us are only too familiar the interest element of each payment will be higher at the start of the lease term as it is calculated on the outstanding balance.

Analytical consequences of the lease decision

		Operating lease	Finance lease
1	Profit margin (early years)	Higher	Lower
2	Profit margin (later years)	Lower	Higher
3	Current ratio	Higher	Lower
4	Gearing	Lower	Higher
5	Return on equity	Higher	Lower
6	Interest coverage	Higher	Lower

1. Profits are adversely effected in the early years of a finance lease as depreciation is coupled with a high interest expense.
2. In later years the pendulum swings as the capital balance outstanding on the finance lease is small leading to greatly reduced interest costs, whereas the operating lease rental remains unchanged.
3. It is usual for lease payments to fall due on a monthly, quarterly or annual basis. These represent liabilities falling due within one year and thereby cause the current ratio of a company employing finance leases to deteriorate.
4. Finance leases recognize the full capital liability at the outset of the lease agreement. This represents a form of long-term finance and causes debt to increase.

   Equity is unaffected as the extra debt is cancelled by the recognition of a fixed asset.
5. In the early years of a finance lease the lowered profits will cause return ratios to deteriorate.
6. Operating lease rentals are treated as an operating expense in the profit and loss account and do not increase the interest cost.

Off-balance-sheet finance

Off-balance-sheet finance has been a much-used term of recent years, and has been closely associated with a number of high-profile corporate frauds.

Operating leases represent an example of off balance sheet finance because unlike a finance lease the outstanding liability for future periods is not recognized on the balance sheet. This is an attractive idea to finance directors looking for legitimate methods to improve key financial indicators, and will work providing the company has net assets rather than net liabilities (Example 15.2).

For evidence of the favourable impact of operating leases on key ratios, refer back to the table in the previous section.

Example 15.2

Off-balance-sheet finance

The finance team of BCD Ltd are trying to explain the benefits of using operating leases over finance leases to other board members. The gross assets of the company are £500,000 and the gross liabilities £200,000.

The machinery they require has a fair value of £100,000, and this can be assumed to be a close approximation to the present value of the minimum lease payments.

NOTE: In practice this is almost certainly a finance lease if we use the 90% test previously described, but for the purpose of this illustration we will assume that it is a borderline decision to illustrate the impact of the two alternatives on the numbers.

If the agreement is treated as a finance lease both assets and liabilities will increase by £100,000 at the outset, whereas an operating lease will leave both assets and liabilities unchanged.

Operating Lease		Finance Lease
£500,000	Assets	£600,000
£200,000	Liabilities	£300,000
£300,000	Equity	£300,000
$\dfrac{200,000}{300,000} = 0.67$	Gearing	$\dfrac{300,000}{300,000} = 1.0$

If the company needed to approach the bank in the future for additional finance it would be preferable for gearing to be lower.

The things every manager must know

1. Operating leases equate to the short-term rental of an asset.
2. Finance leases are an example of commercial substance prevailing over legal form, and as a consequence the leased asset is recognized on the balance sheet of the lessee.
3. Operating leases demonstrate the advantages of off balance sheet finance in the form of improved financial indicators.

Current Assets

A quick recap

The current assets section of the balance normally has three dominant sections, but always be prepared for the odd surprise (Figure 16.1).

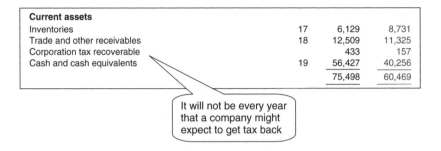

Current assets			
Inventories	17	6,129	8,731
Trade and other receivables	18	12,509	11,325
Corporation tax recoverable		433	157
Cash and cash equivalents	19	56,427	40,256
		75,498	60,469

It will not be every year that a company might expect to get tax back

Figure 16.1 Amstrad plc (2006) – Balance sheet extract

Stock valuation and its impact on financial indicators

Our first step as an analyst should be to refer to the financial statement notes to get a further analysis of this figure.

[*Note*: Inventory is the international equivalent of the term 'stock']

Box 16.1   Amstrad plc (2006) – Inventory note

17. Inventories

	30 June 2006 £'000	30 June 2005 £'000
Finished goods and goods for resale	5,419	8,133
Raw materials and consumables	710	598
	6,129	8,731

Major categories include:

◆ Finished goods
◆ Work in progress

- ◆ Raw materials
- ◆ Consumables.

For some business types, such as house builders, stock will be the most significant number on the balance sheet whereas for an advertising agency it would be insignificant. When stocks are material to the financial statements their impact is pervasive as they have a direct relevance for the balance sheet, cash flow statement and the profit and loss account (remember opening and closing stocks are a key part of cost of sales).

Stock valuation and classification can both be of interest when interpreting the figures. A simple example of the latter relates to consumables which include items such as stationery, wrapping paper and oil for the oil-fired central heating system. The usage of such items would usually be considered an operating expense, but if the core products of the business could not be sold without being wrapped (i.e. it was a prerequisite of sale) then classification as a cost of sale would be more appropriate thereby reducing the gross profit margin of the business.

The core principle of stock valuation is that each major stock category should be valued at the lower of cost and net realizable value. This is another example of the prudence concept as stock should not be included in the balance sheet at more than can be recouped from its sale, but if selling price is higher than cost the profit should not be anticipated.

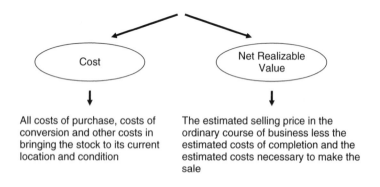

It is important that you have an appreciation of the types of cost that can and cannot be included in stock valuation.

Direct labour	✓
Import duties	✓
Transportation	✓
Trade discount	✓
Early settlement discount	✗

Terminology

Trade discount – This equates to a volume discount whereby a supplier will offer a preferential price for large volume purchases

Early settlement discount – Also known as a cash discount, this has nothing to do with the agreed price at the date of purchase. This discount is offered after the sale by a supplier who is prepared to allow a settlement below the agreed invoice value in exchange for receiving the cash flow earlier.

For low volume businesses such as antique dealers it is possible to track the cost of each unique item brought into stock, but for businesses with high stock volumes this is not possible. A supermarket chain will make daily purchases of similar goods from several suppliers, and it would be impractical to track the individual cost of each item. To assist with this problem there are several cost flow strategies:

◆ FIFO (First In First Out)
◆ Weighted average
◆ LIFO (Last In First Out)

LIFO is prohibited under UK and international GAAP, but is a widely used method in the United States of America.

In periods of inflation the impact of these methods on the reported figures can be dramatic (Example 16.1).

Example 16.1

Cost flow strategies

A company commences trading on 1 January and during the course of the year makes the following purchases of goods for resale.

1 January	200 units	£10 per unit	£2,000
1 March	150 units	£11 per unit	£1,650
1 June	250 units	£13 per unit	£3,250
1 September	200 units	£15 per unit	£3,000
1 December	100 units	£16 per unit	£1,600

| 900 units | | | £11,500 |

At 31 December, 250 units remain in stock. What is the closing stock valuation using FIFO, LIFO and weighted average cost flow strategies.

FIFO

> 100 units at £16 = £1,600
> 150 units at £15 = £2,250

£3,850

LIFO

> 200 units at £10 = £2,000
> 50 units at £11 = £550

£2,250

Weighted average [£11,500/900 = £12.78]

> 250 units at £12.78

£3,195

Based on Example 16.1 it can be appreciated that LIFO is a very prudent method in times of positive inflation as it leaves the oldest, and hence lowest value, stocks in the balance sheet thereby reducing net assets. Simultaneously it includes the most recent, and hence most expensive, stocks in cost of sales thereby reducing the profit for the period.

In contrast FIFO is the least prudent method but is reflective of good stock management as it would be inappropriate to leave perishable goods in the warehouse whilst more recent deliveries were sold in preference.

It should come as no surprise that different cost flow strategies can have a significant impact on financial indicators.

	FIFO	LIFO
Profit margins	Higher	Lower
Asset turnover	Lower	Higher
Current ratio	Higher	Lower
Gearing	Lower	Higher

Long-term contracts – an overview

For most businesses that manufacture their own merchandise for sale the time period an item is classified as work in progress is modest and consequently does not warrant specialist treatment. However, in the case of some construction projects they may take years to complete (e.g. the construction of a new dam or railway tunnel), and this creates a new accounting conundrum.

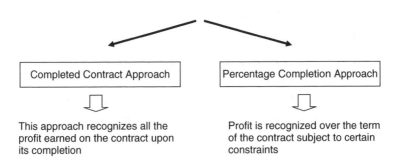

Place yourself in the position of a finance director considering the pros and cons of each approach. Hopefully some of the issues listed below are crystallizing in your mind.

Completed contract approach

♦ Should be straightforward to account for and is a very prudent method.
♦ Ignores the matching principle, whereby costs and revenues are matched to the period in which they are generated.
♦ Creates profit volatility, whereby profits spike in the year of completion although this would be less of an issue for companies with many contracts running concurrently with different completion dates (Figure 16.2).

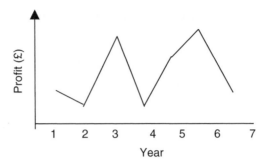

Figure 16.2 The Completed Contracts Approach

Percentage completion approach

◆ Allows the matching concept to prevail over prudence
◆ Generates a smoother profit profile over time.

Best accounting practice recommends that the percentage completion approach be preferred, but this does create additional complexities when trying to understand the story told by the financial statements. Particular considerations include:

> Issue 1 – Should profits be recognized on a long-term contract under all circumstances?

NO – it would be foolish to recognize profits on a large contract if only 1 per cent of the work has been completed, as there would be too much uncertainty about the eventual outcome.

However there is no strict guidance as to the extent of completion before recognition is considered appropriate although there is a broad consensus that 25 per cent is close to the mark.

> Issue 2 – What if a contract is projected to be loss-making?

Prudence must now prevail and the loss should be recognized in full immediately reducing the profits and equity of the business.

> Issue 3 – What is the usual basis for determining the extent of completion and hence the amount of profit that can be recognized in a period?

Contracts of this scale usually have an agreed price, although complications can arise from penalty clauses and so on, and hence the percentage completion can be determined by asking an industry expert to estimate the value of the work completed to date.

	£
Agreed contract price	X
Costs incurred to date	(X)
Estimated future costs of completion	(X)
Estimated total profit	X (say £1,000,000)

If percentage completion is 60 per cent, this implies that 60 per cent of the contract revenues and £600,000 of profit can be recognized (cost of sales will be the balancing figure).

BUT

Remember that some of this revenue/profit may have been recognized in earlier periods and should not be double-counted.

The number of estimates involved in this process would always make this an area for careful review assuming that the figures are material to the financial statements as a whole.

> Issue 4 – Why are long-term contracts of relevance when considering the current assets of the business?

It is unlikely that the actual costs incurred or interim invoices raised will exactly equal the percentage of costs and revenues recognized and the disparities have consequences for the balance sheet.

◆ Actual costs incurred > Cost of sales recognized to date

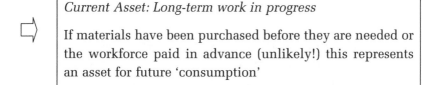

> *Current Asset: Long-term work in progress*
>
> If materials have been purchased before they are needed or the workforce paid in advance (unlikely!) this represents an asset for future 'consumption'

◆ Actual work completed to date > Invoices raised to date

> *Current Asset: Debtor*
>
> Amounts that the business can legitimately invoice

Trade and other debtors

The contents of the debtors section of current assets will differ from company to company, but certain components are common to most. Figure 16.3 gives a typical example of what your examination of the financial statement notes will reveal.

[*Note*: 'Receivables' is the international accounting terminology for debtors]

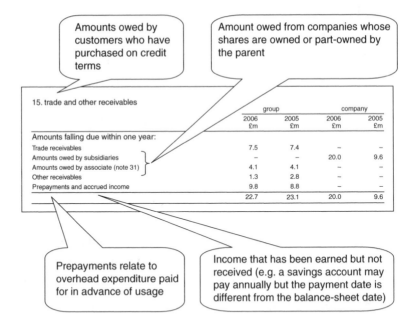

Figure 16.3 Laura Ashley Holdings plc (2006) – Trade and other receivables

When a company is controlled by a parent (remember this represents a subsidiary undertaking) you will note that amounts due are seen in the individual books of the parent, but have disappeared from the group books. We will examine this in more detail when looking at group accounts, but in summary this is because it has been eliminated against a matching liability in the books of the subsidiary.

Bank and cash

In terms of appraising the survival prospects of a business the cash balances are the first port of call, particularly if this can be combined with a cash flow statement which indicates the rate of cash burn by the business.

Cash is an easily understood concept but remember that it includes:

◆ Cash in hand (e.g. petty cash)
◆ Cash held at the bank
◆ Foreign currency
◆ Cash equivalents – these might be disclosed separately on the face of the balance sheet but in most instances you will need to refer to the notes (Box 16.2). They normally represent money market deposits which have less than 3 months to maturity when acquired – they are very liquid and their value is known with accuracy.

Box 16.2 Amstrad plc (2006) – Cash and cash equivalents note

19. Cash and cash equivalents

	30 June 2006 £'000	30 June 2005 £'000
Cash	19,513	17,541
Money market deposits	36,914	22,715
	56,427	40,256

Deposits are treated as cash if they are repayable on demand without notice and without penalties or if they can be withdrawn within 24 hours. Other cash deposits, all of which have a maturity of less than three months, are treated as money market deposits. The credit risk on cash and cash equivalents is limited because the counter parties are banks with high credit ratings assigned by International credit rating agencies. The carrying value of the assets approximates to their fair value.

The things every manager must know

1. Stocks must be valued at the lower of cost and net realizable value.
2. When large volumes of stock are regularly bought and sold it is not practical to identify the unique cost of each unit. In these circumstances cost flow strategies such as LIFO, FIFO and weighted average are used.
3. LIFO is a very prudent stock valuation method but its use is only permitted under US GAAP.
4. Long-term contracts are accounted for using the percentage completion method but profits should not be recognized until the project is sufficiently advanced to enable reasonable estimates of the final outcome to be made.
5. Debtors will include inter-company balances, but balances with subsidiaries will be eliminated in the group financial statements.
6. Cash equivalents maybe included in the cash total as they are highly liquid and their value is known with certainty.

Current Liabilities

Beyond the trade creditor/payable

The balance sheet produced by a company shows a snapshot of assets and liabilities at a point in time. There might be a temptation to believe that the current liabilities were simply trade creditors (known as 'trade payables' under international accounting rules), but the reality is very different, as shown in Box 17.1.

Box 17.1   Woolworths Group plc (2006) – Balance sheet extract

Current liabilities

Financial liabilities

– Borrowings	20	**(90.6)**	(0.1)
– Derivative financial instruments	18	**(22.1)**	–
Trade and other payables	21	**(524.6)**	(552.5)
Current tax liabilities	22	**(12.8)**	(8.8)
Provisions	23	**(12.2)**	(6.3)
		(670.3)	(567.7)

Let us dig a little deeper as some of the items in this section, such as provisions, are subjects upon which our understanding of the true financial position of a business might stand or fall.

Other creditors/payables

Box 17.2 Woolworths Group plc (2006) – Trade and other payables

21. Trade and Other Payables

	28 January 2006 £m	29 January 2005 £m
Current:		
Trade creditors	**251.3**	257.1
Amounts owed to joint ventures	**0.3**	1.8
Other tax and social security	**91.2**	91.2
Other creditors	**69.3**	89.0
Accruals	**112.5**	113.4
	524.6	552.5
Non-current:		
Accruals	**61.8**	50.8
	61.8	50.8

Observations

◆ For most businesses trade creditors will be the dominant figure in this section, and is used by some businesses as a complement to their overall financial strategy. A powerful company might exercise considerable influence over its suppliers, lengthening the time taken to settle invoices in the knowledge that the supplier can ill afford to lose their trade.

◆ When a company has invested in the shares of another to form a group any trading between the companies on credit terms will lead to inter-company balances (i.e. an asset in the books of one and a liability in the books of another). If the investment is designated as a subsidiary (a company controlled by the parent) these balances are reconciled and cancelled when group financial statements are prepared, but when the investment falls short of giving outright control the balances are not eliminated. This can be seen in Box 17.3 with amounts being owed to joint ventures; these are entities subject to shared controll by two or more parties.

- Taxation in all its forms will often be a major outstanding liability of the business. Corporate taxation is often explained separately (i.e. a separate note) leaving outstanding payments for employee tax remitted by the company, national insurance contributions and other taxes.
- Other creditors cover a multitude of possibilities:
  - Interest arrears
  - Dividends declared in the period but unpaid
  - Overdrafts.
- Accruals represent liabilities for the use of utilities and other consumables for which an invoice has yet to be received at the year end but the benefits have already been taken by the company.

UK corporate taxation – a snapshot

In the UK, taxation raised against the profits made by companies is referred to as 'corporation tax' whereas the principal tax on the income of individuals is known as 'income tax'. Confusingly under international accounting rules the tax on both individuals and companies is referred to as 'income tax'.

Dependent upon the size of their profits chargeable to corporation tax a company is designated as a large, small or starter company – the size limits being subject to annual review as part of the budget process undertaken by the Chancellor of the Exchequer. Companies designated as small or medium are required to pay their tax liability 9 months and 1 day after the end of the chargeable accounting period. Large companies pay in four quarterly instalments starting on the 14th day of the 7th month of the accounting period (i.e. before the year has been completed).

In all cases it can be seen that the liability will have fallen due within 1 year of the company's year end and hence will be deemed to be a current liability.

What is deferred income?

It may seem strange to have income as a liability in the balance sheet, but what if income is received in advance for goods or a service that has yet to be rendered?

Under these circumstances the cash received is effectively owed to the customer until the service is provided.

Step 1

| Cash (increases) | Asset |
| Deferred income (increases) | Liability |

Step 2

| Sales (increase) | Service provided |
| Deferred income (decreases) | Eliminating the balance |

Box 17.3 Dairy Crest Group plc – Deferred income note

22 Deferred income

| | **2006** | **2005** |
Current	**£m**	£m
Grants	**1.2**	0.9
Non-current		
Grants	**9.8**	10.7
Other	**0.6**	0.7
	10.4	11.4

Long-term contracts revisited

We have previously examined the nature of long-term contracts and their potential for increasing the current assets of a business, but it is also possible for them to impact current liabilities.

◆ Cost of sales recognized on the contract > Costs invoiced to date

> If the contract is anticipated to be profitable this disparity will be recognized as an accrual, whereas for loss-making contracts it will usually be classified as a provision.

◆ Amounts invoiced to date > Value of work certified to date

> Clearly a liability, in this situation it would also make us query the systems and controls of the business as such poor practice is likely to impact third-party perceptions of the company to its long-term detriment.

Box 17.4 Jarvis plc (2006) – Construction contracts

19.2 Construction contracts

Construction contracts in progress are analysed as follows:	31 March 2006 £m	31 March 2006 £m
Due from customers for contract work included in trade and other receivables	5.4	11.1
Due to customers for contract work included in trade and other payables	(0.3)	(9.3)
	5.1	2.5
Retentions held by customers	1.6	2.5
Aggregate amount of contract costs incurred plus recognised profits less losses to date*	33.8	379.1

* This represents the cumulative amount to date for contracts in progress as at the balance sheet date.

Have the days of big bath provisions really died?

Provisions are often described very differently depending on the contributor.

'The life blood of the creative accountant'

'A necessary evil to be kept to a minimum'

'A crucial element to a full understanding of a business'

'A looking glass to the future'

The truth lies in the combination of all of these statements although every effort has been made by the accounting community to limit the opportunities for manipulating the financial statements. In times gone by large, unnecessary provisions known as big bath provisions would be set up in one period and then released at the discretion of management in future periods to smooth profits or enhance results when required. You might believe that such practice would be easily spotted by readers of the accounts, but this would not always be the case.

◆ The provision could be established in a period when results greatly exceeded expectations. Readers would still perceive the company to be well run and pay little attention to the provision.
◆ Using a reverse psychology provisions were also set up in periods when very poor results were announced thereby concealing the provision as just part of the bad news.
◆ Provisions are by nature one-off events. The expense they represent is often shown as an exceptional item to assist readers in identifying their existence, but this is a double-edged sword as such classification means that some will pay them little heed because they are not indicative of future performance.

In an effort to ensure that provisions are made solely for legitimate reasons three key tests must be applied:

1. An entity has a present obligation, legal or constructive, as a result of a past event.

A legal obligation normally takes the form of a contract whereas a constructive obligation arises from a course of dealing (e.g. a retail store has historically always allowed customers to exchange goods previously purchased although the bill of sale does not obligate them to do so).

> 2. It is probable that an outflow of resources embodying economic benefits will be required to settle the obligation.

The term 'probable' has no exact definition but is often interpreted as implying a probability of more than 50 per cent.

> 3. A reliable estimate can be made of the amount of the obligation.

To understand the application of these rules consider the following examples.

Example 17.1

An onerous lease

On 1 January 2005 RST Ltd entered into a 5-year lease for retail premises. The annual lease rental was £30,000 per annum.

At the end of 2006 the success of the business required them to move to larger premises, but they were unable to sub-let their original premises.

> A provision should be made for the three remaining rentals (i.e. £90,000 – although this is likely to be discounted to its present value).
>
> The past obligating event was signing the lease contract, the payments will have to be made and the amount of each payment is known.

Example 17.2

Environmental damage

GHI Ltd is a natural resources exploration and extraction company. It has made its name on the basis of being environmentally aware and promotes this within its advertising material.

Its most recent survey has been in a country where environmental legislation is poorly developed although the government has indicated that laws will be strengthened in the next year. During the survey a chemical spillage occurred contaminating the ground water supply within a 5 kilometre radius of the site and killing numerous fauna and flora.

> The company has no legal obligation to restore the site and the fact that legislation might be implemented in the near future cannot be anticipated.
>
> Furthermore it will be difficult to quantify the true cost of the contamination.
>
> However, the need for a provision cannot be so easily dismissed as the company may have created a constructive obligation based on the fact that it promotes the business as being environmentally aware!
>
> There is no easy solution to this dilemma and it might ultimately be decided by the company's perception of the financial impact on shareholder value of diminishing the brand.

Although most provisions will be shown within balance-sheet liabilities there are exceptions. The most noteworthy of these are provisions for doubtful debts – effectively the risk of non-receipt of payment from debtors. This provision is usually netted off balance-sheet debtors. This type of provision always causes some anxiety as there is no argument about making a provision against a named debtor account (e.g. because they are known to be in financial difficulties), but companies will also make a general provision in anticipation of bad news as yet undiscovered. The latter is usually a percentage of the total debtor balance and appears to transgress the provisioning rules about both anticipation of future events and measurability. However, if the level of provisioning is consistently applied, and retrospective review demonstrates that this is not excessive in proportion to the number of payment defaults, it will be tolerated.

The future of provisioning – a technical moment

To complement your growing repertoire of financial knowledge and skills it is useful to be aware of major changes that may occur to best accounting practice in the future. Provisioning is one such area where there are plans to change the rules.

The proposed definition of a provision is:

> a present obligation of the entity arising from past events, the settlement of which is expected to result in an outflow from the entity of resources embodying economic benefits

At first glance this appears to be a similar definition to that which is currently employed, but there is a key difference. All reference to probability has been removed with the likely consequence that if the new rules take effect companies will be required to recognize a greater number of provisions.

Financial instruments – a warning shot

Reference back to Box 17.1 will highlight a financial liabilities section within current liabilities. This is a consequence of the introduction of new rules on financial instruments, but is a subject matter covered in later sections which look at the consequences of financing decisions taken by management.

The things every manager must know

1. Trade creditors are just one element of liabilities falling due within 1 year which also encapsulates outstanding interest and dividends, taxation, provisions and so on.
2. Big bath provisioning has been curtailed by more stringent rules on provisioning, but the inherent uncertainty attached to the need for a provision means that some creative accounting is still possible.
3. Deferred income represents money received by the company, and for which it has not provided the services or goods at the balance-sheet date.

Company Financing

Debt vs. equity

Successful companies want to grow by acquisition or by inward investment in long-term projects, poorly performing companies need funds to see them through the hard times and companies holding the status quo need to replace fixed assets. The bottom line is that none of these activities can usually be covered by cash flows from operating activities alone, there is a requirement for a longer-term injection of finance.

These additional funds can be raised either from the issue of additional shares or from borrowing and this crucial decision has wide-ranging implications for the financial statements. You will remember that the interest payments on debt are tax deductible but have the downside that they cannot be avoided, whereas dividend payments are at the discretion of management but as an appropriation of profits to shareholders are not tax deductible.

Ignoring the tax deductible nature of interest the cost of debt is usually lower than the cost of equity because lenders are exposed to less risk than the providers of equity finance. Lenders will be paid in priority to shareholders should the company be wound up, and they often secure their position with charges over the company assets or in the case of small companies via personal guarantees from the directors (a feature that casts a shadow over the concept of limited liability).

A company that has a high level of debt to equity is said to be highly geared, and may find it difficult to raise additional finance particularly if profits are sensitive to relatively small changes in sales thereby increasing the risk of interest default. It should come as no surprise that companies whose management team is gearing sensitive will try to adopt strategies that minimize the perceived danger. Based on the accounting principles reviewed so far consider what strategies you might adopt to achieve this objective – they could include:

◆ Adoption of off-balance-sheet finance strategies such as the use of operating leases.
◆ Revision of accounting estimates such as the useful economic life of fixed assets to reduce the depreciation expense, increase profits and thereby increase equity.
◆ Selection of accounting policies that maximize equity such as the upward revaluation of assets where circumstances allow.

Preference share capital

Preference shares represent a unique challenge to the reviewer of financial information, and to understand the reason why we need to consider the key features usually attributed to these instruments.

1. Preference shareholders get a fixed dividend (e.g. 5% of the nominal value of the share).
2. If a company fails to pay the preference dividend then it normally accrues for payment in later period.
3. Preference shareholders do not have the right to vote unless dividends are in arrears.
4. If the company is wound up the preference shareholders get paid in priority to the ordinary shareholders but after settlement of bank liabilities and trade creditors.
5. Capital returns to preference shareholders are restricted to the par value of the share.

In calculating the gearing ratio for a business there is a dilemma – should preference shares be treated as debt or equity?

Traditionally analysts have treated them as debt, but national company law (e.g. UK company legislation) requires disclosure in the equity section of the balance sheet. International accounting practice addresses this issue and is being more widely adopted although the transition is not always smooth because in certain countries it necessitates changes to legislation so that the law and best accounting practice do not conflict. In summary the recommended international accounting treatment is:

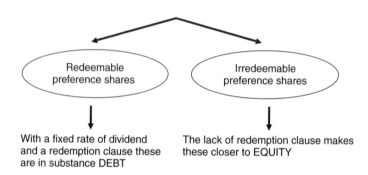

So much more than a loan

For many companies the nature of the debt in their balance sheet is relatively simple – namely a loan from the bank or similar financial institution, and reference to the financial statement notes will give an analysis of the repayment schedule. This is particularly useful as it gives early warning of potential pressure points on the company cash flows (Box 18.1).

Box 18.1 easyJet plc (2005) – Loans note

15. Loans

	2005 **£million**	2004 £million
Amounts falling due:		
Within one year	**16.3**	9.7
Due within one to two years	**17.0**	10.1
Due in two to five years	**68.4**	37.2
Due after five years	**118.7**	62.8
	220.4	119.8
Less deferred financing costs	**(3.1)**	—
	217.3	119.8
Included within amounts falling due within one year	**(16.3)**	(9.7)
	201.0	110.1

The bank loans financed the acquisition of certain aircraft by the Group. The aircraft acquired with the loans are provided as security against the borrowings.

Interest and repayment terms and also maturity details for the bank loans are set out in note 23.

Unfortunately for independent users of financial statements larger companies are becoming evermore inventive in the types of arrangement used to raise finance, and this has required the accounting profession to demand evermore comprehensive disclosures and accounting treatments to ensure that meaningful comparisons can be made. It is not the intention of this book to explore in depth complex financing strategies as that is the domain of specialists rather than those trying to get a broad understanding of financial information, but it would be a shame not to move the door slightly ajar so that you have an awareness of the issues.

Welcome to the new world of financial instruments

A financial instrument is defined as:

> Any contract that gives rise to a financial asset of one entity and a financial liability or equity instrument of another

Although this is clearly a very wide-ranging definition it does not in itself look that daunting, but the complexity comes from the complex nature of financing strategies and associated instruments now used by some companies, particularly those in the financial sector.

Accounting guidance now allocates financial assets and liabilities into several categories, and each item must be designated at origination with subsequent reclassification only allowed in rare circumstances. The significance of the classification is that different accounting treatments are associated with each category and this can have a significant impact on the financial statements.

Financial assets

Assets at fair value through profit or loss	Typically this category includes financial assets held for trading.
	They are revalued to their fair value and the increase or decrease in value is taken through the profit and loss account.
	A potential criticism of this method is that it creates profit volatility, but conceptually this is seen as the ideal method in that it reflects true values to the users of the financial statements.

Loans and receivables	These are assets with fixed or determinable payments that are not quoted in an active market and do not qualify as trading assets.
	These are accounted for using a method called 'amortized cost' (Example 18.1).
Held-to-maturity investments	These are assets with fixed and determinable payments and a fixed maturity, other than loans and receivables, for which there is a positive intention and ability to hold to maturity.
	These are also accounted for using the amortized cost approach.
Available-for-sale	A default category for assets that do not belong in one of the other three categories of financial asset.
	These are remeasured to their fair value but the movement is not taken directly to the profit and loss account. Instead the movements are taken to the reserves in the balance sheet, until the asset is sold or suffers an impairment in value. When this trigger event occurs the accumulated movements are recycled through the face of the profit and loss account.

Financial liabilities

| Liabilities at fair value through profit or loss | As with their asset counterparts these are revalued to their fair value and the movement taken to the face of the profit and loss account. |
| Other financial liabilities | These are accounted for using a method called 'amortized cost' (Example 18.1). |

Example 18.1

Understanding the accounting implications of amortized cost

WXY plc needs to raise additional finance, and has taken the decision to issue a bond to generate the additional cash. The bond has a face value of £1,000,000 and carries an annual coupon rate of 4 per cent.

NOTE: The term 'coupon rate' refers to the interest payments the bond holder will receive based on the face value of the bond, and not the price at which it trades.

The coupon offered is the maximum the company can sustain given its current cash flows, but this is below market rates making the bond unattractive. To compensate the bond is issued for £800,000, but will be redeemed in 5 years at its face value.

Costs associated with issuing the bond were £11,184.

The bond is classified as an 'other liability' and is to be accounted for using amortized cost.

To understand amortized cost it is important to identify the true finance cost of the bond to WXY plc

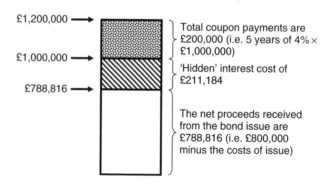

The £411,184 difference between the net proceeds and the total cash paid to the bond holder over the term of the bond is the true finance cost, and this equates to a compound interest rate of 9.5 per cent per annum.

The bond is initially recorded in the accounts of the company at the value of the net proceeds received.

Cash (increase)	£788,816
Bond (increase)	£788,816

Subsequent accounting entries are derived from the completion of an amortized cost schedule

Year	Amount Borrowed £	Interest [9.5%] £	Repayment [4% Coupon] £	Amount Due £
1	788,816	74,938	(40,000)	823,754
2	823,754	78,257	(40,000)	862,011
3	862,011	81,891	(40,000)	903,902
4	903,902	85,870	(40,000)	949,772
5	949,772	90,228	(40,000)	1,000,000

At the end of year 1 the consequences for the financial statements would be:

Interest expense (increase)	£74,938
Cash (decrease)	£40,000
Bond (increase)	£34,938

Hence at the end of the year the carrying value of the liability in the balance sheet has increased – some of the interest expense is said to have been 'rolled up' into the carrying value of the bond. The knock-on effects of these entries are considerable:

◆ Interest cover is reduced as £74,938 is recognized as interest instead of the £40,000 coupon.
◆ Gearing deteriorates as the balance liability increases in conjunction with the reduced profits having a detrimental impact on equity.

At the end of the 5-year term the carrying value of the bond equates to its redemption price and the liability outstanding to the bond holder will be settled.

Bond (decrease)	£1,000,000
Cash (decrease)	£1,000,000

In year 5 the bond will also be reclassified as a liability falling due within 1 year.

Are the new rules necessary?

At first glance the raft of new accounting rules on financial instruments and the extensive disclosure requirements which accompany them may seem too onerous. Remember that financial statements are supposed to assist the reader in understanding the performance and position of the business.

However, we need to keep both a sense of proportion and look at the alternatives.

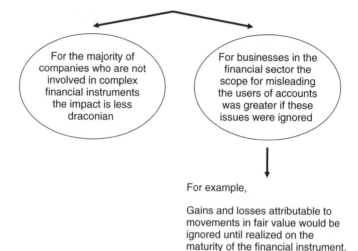

For the majority of companies who are not involved in complex financial instruments the impact is less draconian

For businesses in the financial sector the scope for misleading the users of accounts was greater if these issues were ignored

For example,

Gains and losses attributable to movements in fair value would be ignored until realized on the maturity of the financial instrument. If these movements were large it might have come as a nasty shock to an investor if they have not had some early warning in the form of recognizing movements accrued at each previous period end.

Convertible debt

Convertible debt represents a debt instrument which includes an option for the holder to convert the debt into shares at a later date(s). The inclusion of this additional right often means that the company can offer a slightly lower interest return on the instrument as the debt holder has the possibility of making an additional large return in the future if the market price of the shares is high.

The key question is should convertible debt be treated as debt or equity – a vital question when linked to covenants such as gearing. Historically the view has been not to anticipate conversion, but under the new financial instrument rules convertible debt is now split.

Using discounted cash flow techniques the interest payment and final redemption value are discounted back to their present value and classified as debt. Any remaining balance is then treated as equity in accordance with the rule which says that equity will always be the residual.

The things every manager must know

1. There are two principal methods of financing the long-term activities of a business – debt and equity.
2. Debt is cheaper than equity as the finance cost is tax deductible, but excess debt is frowned upon as the interest payments cannot be avoided in good times or bad.
3. Redeemable preference shares share most of the attributes associated with debt and should be classified as such. Irredeemable preference shares will be classified as equity.
4. Additional information on the debt profile of a business can be found in the financial statement notes.
5. Large financial institutions and public companies are finding increasingly varied and complex methods by which to finance their activities. This has been addressed by the accounting world with extensive new rules that categorize financial instruments and provide unique accounting treatments for each.
6. In the long term there is a drive to the more extensive use of fair value accounting so that the users of financial statements will be able to see the true value of financial instruments in the balance sheet.
7. Convertible debt must be split into its component parts of debt and equity.

Further Clues about the Future of the Business

Contingencies

Contingencies can be viewed as potential assets or liabilities dependent upon the outcome of a specific event which has not been concluded at the balance-sheet date. A typical example is a legal case pending against a company which has yet to come to court.

The accounting treatment for contingencies is linked to the probability of a given outcome, but with additional prudence being shown towards contingent assets in keeping with best practice. The rules under UK and international GAAP can be summarized as follows:

Probability of outcome	Contingent Asset	Contingent Liability
Remote	Ignore	Ignore
Possible	Ignore	Disclose in notes
Probable	Disclose in notes	Make a provision

Sadly there is no watertight guidance on the meaning of the terms probable, possible and remote leaving scope for creative accounting. However, in spite of this reservation the additional disclosures given in the notes can give a useful insight into the dangers that might lie ahead.

As a rough guide the term 'probable' is said to imply a probability of more than 50%, but what criteria will be used to quantify this benchmark?

Box 19.1 easyJet plc (2005) – Contingencies note

20. Contingent liabilities

The Group is involved in various disputes or litigation in the normal course of business. Whilst the result of such disputes cannot be predicted with certainty, the Company believes that the ultimate resolution of these disputes will not have a material affect on the Group's financial position or results.

In 2002, Navitaire Inc., a former supplier of airline reservation software to easyJet Airline Company Limited, a Group company, issued proceedings against that Group company alleging copyright infringement in relation to airline reservations software. In November 2005, the parties reached an amicable agreement fully resolving the dispute, bringing the litigation to an end.

Box 19.2   Woolworths Group plc (2006) – Contingencies note

34. Contingent Liabilities

On the formation of 2entertain Limited, Woolworths Group agreed to guarantee a stipulated level of profitability for certain key VCI contracts in the event that any such contracts terminated during a period of three years to September 2007, No liability was incurred in respect of year one and a provision of £5.2 million has been recognised in respect of years two and three, against a potential maximum exposure for the two remaining years of £7.8 million. Based on results to date no further provision is required, however the future performance of these contracts is uncertain.

In common with a number of retailers Woolworths Group has challenged HM Revenue & Customs on the recoverability of VAT on merchant services. Following the Court of Appeal decision in July 2005 no repayment will arise to the Group. Certain matters relating to merchant services remain to be resolved, but based on advice taken, it is considered that no material liability will be incurred. However this is not certain. As at the balance sheet date no provision has been made.

Post-balance-sheet events

The wheels of commerce relentlessly turn and hence it is inevitable that events will continue to occur after the date on which the financial statements are prepared. Initially you might simply shrug your shoulders and make statements such as:

"That's a matter for next year's financial statements"

"Best accounting practice does not allow the recognition of future events"

These statements are fundamentally correct, but it would be irresponsible to leave the story here.

What if a matter was drawn to the attention of the finance director several weeks after the balance sheet date, but related to circumstances which existed at that date?

Example 19.1

Adjusting post-balance-sheet events

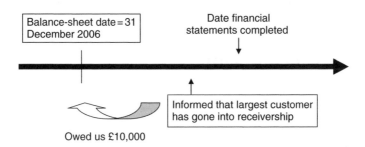

It is unlikely that the customer was a vibrant and successful business at our balance-sheet date and yet has failed only a few weeks later. The reality is that had we investigated at 31 December 2006 evidence would have been found of their financial difficulties and a provision made against the possibility of non-collectability of the debt.

Under these circumstances the 2006 financial statements should be adjusted to include the provision. This is not an anticipation of the future, but simply the recognition of facts that already existed but had previously gone unnoticed.

The nature of post-balance-sheet events means that they are unique to that business, but Box 19.3 provides an excellent example of the type of information to be found.

> **Box 19.3**   easyJet plc (2005) – Post-balance-sheet events note
>
> **25. Post balance sheet events**
>
> David Bennett was appointed to the Board as a Non-Executive Director on 1 October 2005.
>
> One Boeing 737-300 aircraft was transferred from fixed assets to debtors in September 2005 as a contract had been signed for its sale. The aircraft was delivered in November 2005.
>
> In 2002, Navitaire Inc., a former supplier of airline reservation software to easyJet Airline Company Limited, a Group company, issued proceedings against that Group company alleging copyright infringement in relation to airline reservations software. In November 2005, the parties reached an amicable agreement fully resolving the dispute, bringing the litigation to an end.

Capital commitments

When deciding on the future strategy of a business a useful insight is obtained if we know of major investments to which they are committed or obligations from which they cannot escape. This is the role of the capital commitments note found in many financial statements.

Typically the note highlights two pieces of information and this is demonstrated by Box 19.4.

1. An analysis is provided of operating lease commitments. This is informative but great care needs to be taken regarding its interpretation. Under UK GAAP (i.e. as per Box 19.4) this shows the obligations for the next accounting period analysed by the unexpired term of the lease.

   Under international GAAP this note shows the total future obligation under operating leases analysed by when they fall due.

Box 19.4   easyJet plc (2005) – Commitments note

21. Commitments

a) Lease commitments Non-cancellable commitments under operating leases to pay rentals during the year following the year end analysed according to the period in which each lease expires were as follows:

	Land and buildings	
	2005	2004
	£million	£million
Expiring less than one year	**0.4**	0.2
Expiring between two and five years	**0.1**	0.3
Expiring after more than five years	**0.4**	0.1
	0.9	0.6

	Aircraft	
	2005	2004
	£million	£million
Expiring less than one year	**13.9**	6.2
Expiring between two and five years	**31.3**	50.7
Expiring after more than five years	**102.7**	43.2
	147.9	100.1

b) Other financial commitments. As a result of a purchase agreement approved by shareholders in March 2003, the Group is contractually committed to the acquisition of a further 65 new Airbus A319 aircraft with a list price of approximately US $2.9 billion, being approximately £1.6 billion (before escalations, discounts and deposit payments already made). In respect of those aircraft, deposit payments amounting to US $262.0 million or £148.1 million (2004: US $299.4 million or £165.4 million) had been made as at 30 September 2005, for commitments for the acquisition of Airbus A319 aircraft.

At 30 September 2005 the Group had placed a series of orders to purchase aircraft spare parts, totalling approximately £nil (2004: £1.1 million).

2. All other capital commitments are briefly described. These are assets which the business has undertaken to purchase but has not yet acquired and brought into use. This information can assist a reviewer to further understand the business in a number of ways:
   - ◆ Timing of future cash demands
   - ◆ Management ambition to expand the existing business or to enter new markets.

Multi-year analysis

Public companies (i.e. those listed on a public exchange) are required to provide a summary of their results not just for the previous period but for several years (e.g. 5 years in the UK).

This is a vital resource if we are to understand more about the historic performance of the business, and use this as a tool to help predict what the future might hold. Some companies provide this information in the form of a detailed analysis of revenue and expenses (Box 19.5) whilst others provide key financial indicators (Box 19.6) – both of which are valuable.

Box 19.5 Halfords Group plc (2006) – 5-year summary of results
Five Year Record

	52 weeks to 29 March 2002 £m UK GAAP*	52 weeks to 28 March 2003 £m UK GAAP*	53 weeks to 2 April 2004 £m UK GAAP†	52 weeks to 1 April 2005 £m IFRS	52 weeks to 31 March 2006 £m IFRS
Revenue	519.8	525.8	578.6	628.4	681.7
Cost of sales	(243.3)	(244.4)	(271.6)	(292.0)	(335.0)
Gross profit	276.5	281.4	307.0	336.4	346.7
Operating expenses	(225.0)	(247.9)	(244.1)	(247.1)	(257.6)
Operating profit before exceptional items and goodwill amortisation	51.5	50.8	70.0	89.5	89.1
Goodwill amortisation	—	(8.0)	(13.7)	—	—
Exceptional items	—	(9.3)	—	(0.2)	—
Operating profit	51.5	33.5	62.9	89.3	89.1
Loss on sale of business	(2.3)	—	—	—	—
Profit on sale of fixed assets	—	—	0.4	—	—

Net finance costs	(0.5)	(21.9)	(44.1)	(15.0)	(12.1)
Profit before tax	48.7	11.6	25.2	74.3	77.0
Tax	(16.7)	(6.5)	(14.3)	(23.2)	(23.4)
Profit attributable to equity shareholders	32.0	5.1	10.9	51.1	53.6
Basic earnings per share	n/a	n/a	6.7p	23.7p	23.6p
Basic earnings per share before goodwill amortisation and exceptional items	n/a	n/a	16.1p	23.7p	23.6p

* as previously reported

† restated

Halfords Group plc acquired Halfords Limited on 30 August 2002. Prior to this date, Halfords Limited was a wholly owned subsidiary of Boots Group plc and therefore, prior to 30 August 2002, the financial information above is based on the financial statements of Halfords Limited, In June 2004, Halfords Group plc listed on the London Stock Exchange. Consequently, the results across the periods reflect the differences in the capital and financing structure under the different ownerships.

An analysis of the main differences between UK GAAP and IFRS are detailed in note 25 to the financial statements.

Box 19.6 Barratt Developments plc (2005) – 5-year summary of results

Five Year Record and Financial Calendar

FIVE YEAR RECORD					
Year	2005	2004	2003 Restated	2002 Restated	2001 Restated
Group turnover £m	2,512.7	2,516.0	2,171.0	1,799.4	1,509.1
Profit before tax £m	406.6	367.7	288.7	220.0	178.4
Share capital and reserves £m	1,352.0	1,116.1	908.9	741.8	619.4
Per ordinary share:					
Earnings (basic) pence	123.6	111.4	89.1	68.6	55.1
Dividend pence	26.98	21.58	17.26	14.38	13.07
Net assets pence	559	465	381	312	264
Dividend cover	4.6	5.2	5.2	4.8	4.2

As with most financial information these summaries come with a health warning.

◆ Performance trends of the past 5 years are no guarantee as to what the future holds
◆ Modest improvements in turnover and so on may not be reflective of improvement in times of positive inflation, but is simply an indicator of holding the status quo. It is better to calculate key ratios to understand if the business is really improving.

Segmental analysis

Imagine that you have been presented with the following information for an international conglomerate:

	Year 1	Year 2	Year 3	Year 4	Year 5
	£m	£m	£m	£m	£m
Turnover	45	55	46	54	?
Profit after taxation	4.7	4.9	4.3	5.0	?

If asked to predict the turnover and profit after taxation for year 5 this would prove an almost impossible task given the fluctuations of recent history. However, the task would be made easier if the following information was also made available.

Turnover

	Year 1	Year 2	Year 3	Year 4	Year 5
	£m	£m	£m	£m	£m
Europe	22.6	26.6	15.3	17.8	
Africa	15.6	19.8	21.1	24.4	
Asia	6.8	8.6	9.6	11.8	
Total	45	55	46	54	?

Both Africa and Asia appear to be sustaining positive growth. Europe is also growing but after a dramatic downturn in trade following year 2.

Profit after taxation

	Year 1	Year 2	Year 3	Year 4	Year 5
	£m	£m	£m	£m	£m
Europe	1.5	1.3	0.5	0.8	
Africa	2.2	2.6	2.9	3.4	
Asia	1.0	1.0	0.9	0.8	
Total	4.7	4.9	4.3	5.0	?

Although the Asian market is growing in volume it appears to be at the expense of profit margin. Questions we would ask of management include:

- Have prices been cut to promote sales?
- Has the cost base of the Asian market been inflated, possibly by increased marketing costs?

The African market seems to be the best performing market. It has shown steady growth in turnover and profit and is now the largest contributor to the group. If these profits are backed by positive cash flows then this market is disproportionately significant, but we may question if it is reaching a ceiling which might curtail future expectations.

The European market is showing modest signs of recovery following the trauma suffered in year 3.

Overall it can be seen that the provision of segmental information can greatly increase our understanding of the business, and enhance our ability to make future projections. Listed companies are required to give segmental information in their published accounts, and a typical example can be seen in Box 19.7.

Box 19.7 Vodafone plc (2006) – Segmental analysis extract

3. Segmental analysis

The Group's business is principally the supply of mobile telecommunications services and products. Primary segmental information is provided on the basis of geographic regions, being the basis on which the Group manages its worldwide interests. Other operations primarily comprise fixed line telecommunications businesses. The segmental analysis is provided for the Group's continuing operations. Revenue is determined by location of assets, which is not materially different from revenue by location of customer. Inter-segment sales are charged at arms length prices.

| | Mobile telecommunications | | | | | | | | Other operations | | Group |
| | Germany | Italy | Spain | UK | US | Other mobile | Common function | Total | Germany | Other | |
	£m	£m	£m	£m	£m	£m	£m	£m	£m	£m	£m
31 March 2006											
Service revenue	5,394	4,170	3,615	4,568	–	8,530		26,277	1,320	19	27,616
Equipment and other revenue	360	193	380	480	–	720		2,133	–	–	2,133
Segment revenue	5,754	4,363	3,995	5,048	–	9,250		28,410	1,320	19	29,749
Subsidiaries	5,754	–	3,995	5,048	–	7,812		22,609	1,320	–	23,929
Joint ventures	–	4,363	–	–	–	1,470		5,833	–	19	5,852
Less: inter-segment revenue	–	–	–	–	–	(32)		(32)	–	–	(32)
Common functions							145	145			145
Inter-segment revenue	(64)	(44)	(105)	(65)	–	(121)	(19)	(418)	–	–	(418)

Net revenue	5,690	4,319	3,890	4,983	—	9,129	126	28,137	1,320	19	29,476
Less: revenue between mobile and other operations	(91)	—	—	—	—	(1)	—	(92)	(34)	—	(126)
Group revenue	5,599	4,319	3,890	4,983	—	9,128	126	28,045	1,286	19	29,350
Segment result	(17,904)	(1,928)	968	698	—	1,296	—	(16,870)	139	4	(16,727)
Subsidiaries	(17,904)	—	968	698	—	933	—	(15,305)	139	—	(15,166)
Joint ventures	—	(1,928)	—	—	—	363	—	(1,565)	—	4	(1,561)
Common functions							215	215			215
Share of result in associated undertakings	—	—	—	—	1,732	712	8	2,452	—	(24)	2,428
Operating (loss)/profit	(17,904)	(1,928)	968	698	1,732	2,008	223	(14,203)	139	(20)	(14,084)
Non-operating income and expense											(2)
Investment income											353
Financing costs											(1,120)
Loss before taxation											(14,853)
Tax on loss											(2,380)
Loss for the year from continuing operations											(17,233)
Operating loss	(17,904)	(1,928)	968	698	1,732	2,008	223	(14,203)	139	(20)	(14,084)
Add back:											
Impairment losses	19,400	3,600	—	—	—	515	—	23,515	—	—	23,515
Non-recurring items related to acquisitions and disposals	—	—	—	—	—	(20)	(12)	(32)	—	—	(32)

Commercial Awareness and Business Decision-Making Skills

Adjusted operating profit	1,496	1,672	968	698	1,732	2,503	211	9,280	139	(20)	9,399
Non-current assets[1]	24,360	19,422	12,596	8,743	–	17,200	1,907	84,228	754	64	85,046
Investment in associated undertakings	–	–	–	–	17,898	5,182	37	23,117	–	80	23,197
Current assets[1]	669	888	443	743	–	1,555	79	4,377	266	13	4,656
Total segment assets[1]	25,029	20,310	13,039	9,486	17,898	23,937	2,023	111,722	1,020	157	112,899
Unallocated non-current assets:											
Deferred tax assets											140
Trade and other receivables											231
Unallocated current assets:											
Cash and cash equivalents											2,789
Trade and other receivables											79
Taxation recoverable											8
Assets included in disposal group for resale[2]											10,592
Total assets											126,738

Notes:

(1) Excluding unallocated items.

(2) See note 29 for information on discontinued operations.

The exact nature of the disclosures required varies depending upon the GAAP used to prepare the financial statements, but common ground will include:

♦ Analysis by business type and geographical activity
♦ Sufficient information on profits and net assets to enable key financial indicators such as return on capital employed to be calculated for each major segment.

This is particularly useful when trying to understand if investment capital has been directed towards those elements of the business likely to generate the best return.

The things every manager must know

1. The treatment of a contingent event is dependent on a combination of the probability of occurrence and prudence.
2. Events occurring after the balance-sheet date are adjusted for if they relate to circumstances in existence at the balance-sheet date.
3. The capital commitments note gives a useful insight of future capital expenditure and contracted payments under the terms of operating leases.
4. Listed companies are required to provide a 5-year historic summary of results and a segmental analysis based on business and geographical criteria. This information allows trends to be identified and more accurate predictions to be made about the future.

Things You Always Wanted to Know But Were Afraid to Ask

Related parties

When considering the results of a company as portrayed by its financial statements it would be reasonable to assume that the transactions summarized therein represented transactions that had been conducted at arms length between independent parties. If this is not true then you would like to know as this would make you reappraise the information and its validity for decision-making.

> Example: Imagine trading between two companies controlled by members of the same family. There is increased scope for the inter-company transactions not to be at fair value thereby distorting margins and returns.

At this point it should be recognized that there is both good and bad news for the potential reviewer.

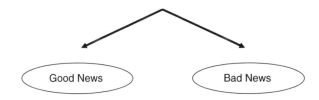

Good News	Bad News
Companies are required to give additional disclosures identifying what are know as RELATED PARTY relationships	If a management team wanted to conceal a related party relationship from investors and the auditors it can be difficult to establish their existence

Typical examples of related parties include:

◆ Parties that control, are controlled by, or are under the common control with, the entity.
   This is primarily focussed on groups of companies.

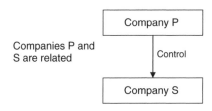

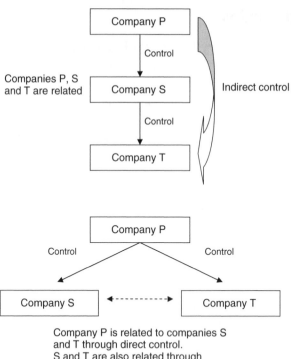

Companies P, S and T are related

Company P

Control

Company S

Control

Company T

Indirect control

Company P

Control

Control

Company S ◀- - - - - - - -▶ Company T

Company P is related to companies S
and T through direct control.
S and T are also related through
common control

◆ Parties that have significant influence over the entity
   Again this is most common in a group situation. An asso-
   ciate is a company over which another can exert significant
   influence
◆ Parties that have joint control over the entity
◆ Key management personnel
◆ Close family members.
   There is no precise dividing line as to which family members this
   would include, but the key lies in the ability to exert influence.

To avoid making related party disclosures too onerous companies
are not automatically related simply because they have a director in common. Similarly customers and suppliers are not related
parties simply because a large volume of business is conducted
with them.

Disclosure is given of the related parties and the nature of the transactions between them (Boxes 20.1 and 20.2).

Box 20.1 British Airways plc (2006) – Related party disclosure note

33. Related party transactions

The Group and Company had transactions in the ordinary course of business during the year under review with related parties.

	Group		Company	
£ million	2006	*2005*	2006	*2005*
Associates:				
Sales to associates	54	*47*	53	*47*
Purchases from associates	149	*137*	146	*137*
Amounts owed to associates	10	*9*	10	*9*
Subsidiaries:				
Sales to subsidiaries			84	*87*
Purchases from subsidiaries			116	*107*
Amounts owed by subsidiaries			112	*234*
Amounts owed to subsidiaries			1,827	*1,844*

In addition, the Company meets certain costs of administering the Group's retirement benefit plans, including the provision of support services to the Trustees. Costs borne on behalf of the retirement benefit plans amounted to £1.4 million in relation to the costs of the Pension Protection Fund levy (2005: nil).

Associates:

Iberia, Lineas Aéreas de España, S.A. ('Iberia')

A 90 per cent owned subsidiary in the Group has a 10 per cent investment in Iberia. Areas of opportunity for co-operation have been identified, and work continues to pursue and implement these. Sales and purchases between related parties are made at normal market prices and outstanding balances are unsecured and interest free and cash settlement is expected within the standard settlement terms specified by the IATA Clearing House.

As at 31 March 2006, the net trading balance owed by the Group to Iberia amounted to £0.4 million (2005: £0.3 million).

Comair Limited

The Group has an 18.3 per cent investment in Comair and has a franchise agreement with the company that commenced in October 1996. Sales and purchases between related parties are made at normal market prices and outstanding balances are unsecured and interest free and cash settlement is expected within the standard settlement terms specified by the IATA Clearing House.

As at 31 March 2006, the net trading balance due to Comair amounted to £9 million (2005: £8 million).

Subsidiaries:

Transactions with subsidiaries are carried out on an arm's length basis. Outstanding balances that relate to trading balances are placed on inter-company accounts with no specified credit period. Long-term loans owed to and from the Company by subsidiary undertakings bear market rates of interest in accordance with the inter-company loan agreements.

Directors' and officers' loans and transactions

No loans or credit transactions were outstanding with directors or officers of the Company at the end of the year or arose during the year that need to be disclosed in accordance with the requirements of Schedule 6 to the Companies Act 1985.

In addition to the above, the Group and Company also have transactions with related parties which are conducted in the normal course of airline business. These include the provision of airline and related services.

Neither the Group nor Company have provided or benefited from any guarantees for any related party receivables or payables. During the year ended 31 March 2006 the Group has not, made any provision for doubtful debts relating to amounts owed by related parties (2005: nil).

Box 20.2 Wilson Bowden plc (2006) – Related party disclosure note

25. Related party transactions

Transactions between the Company and its subsidiaries, which are related parties, have been eliminated on consolidation and are not disclosed.

Remuneration of key personnel

The remuneration of the Directors and other members of the Group's Executive Committee, who are the key management personnel of the Group, is set out below in aggregate for each of the categories specified in IAS24 'Related Party Disclosures'. Further information about the remuneration of individual directors is provided in the audited part of the Directors' Remuneration Report on pages 41 to 43.

	2005 £'000	2004 £'000
Short term employee benefits	4,133	4,149
Post-employment benefits	676	626
Termination benefits	422	–
Total remuneration of key personnel	5,231	4,775

When reviewing related party disclosures it is important to recognize that in the majority of cases the company is not highlighting that transactions have occurred at non-commercial rates, but simply making the reader aware of the relationship because there would be a perception that if economic conditions dictated there would be an increased danger of favouritism to or from such a party.

Deferred taxation and associated tax issues

Deferred taxation is a subject that has long exercised the minds of the accounting profession, and it is not necessary for us to become involved in the technical arguments that exist on this subject. However, it is useful to have an understanding of the key principle involved.

Consider the following profit and loss account extract:

	£
Sales	10,000
Cost of sales	(4,000)
Gross profit/(loss)	**6,000**
Distribution costs	(500)
Administrative expenses	(2,500)
Operating profit/(loss)	**3,000**
Finance cost	(200)
Profit before tax	**2,800**

If informed that the rate of taxation applicable to this company was 30 per cent it would appear reasonable to assume that the tax charge for the year would be £840 (i.e. 30% × £2,800). Consequently it would come as something of a surprise to be informed that the actual figure is £230 or £1125.

The logic for this disparity arises from three sources.

1. When the tax is calculated for a given year the profit figure has often not been finalized leading to an under or overprovision of the tax charge. This is adjusted for in the following year resulting in an aggregate charge that does not match a precise percentage of the stated profit.
2. Subject to certain limitations tax rules often allow losses made in one period to be carried forward and be offset against future profits thereby reducing the apparent rate of tax in that year.

Box 20.3 Newcastle United plc (2005) – Taxation note

7. Taxation

	2005 £'000	2004 £'000
UK corporation tax on profit for the year	–	–
Share of joint venture's tax	**(23)**	55
Total current tax (credit)/charge	**(23)**	55
Deferred tax (note 18)	**143**	–
Tax on profit on ordinary activities	**120**	55

Factors affecting the tax (credit)/charge
for the current period
The current tax credit is lower
(2004: charge lower) than the standard
rate of corporation tax in the UK
of 30% (2004: 30%).
The differences are explained below:

	2005 £'000	2004 £'000
Current tax reconciliation		
Profit on ordinary activities before tax	16	4,220
Current tax at 30% (2004: 30%)	5	1,266
Effects of:		
Expenses not deductible for tax purposes	619	901
Depreciation for year less than capital allowances	(110)	(437)
Other timing differences	436	343
Utilisation of tax losses	(973)	(2,018)
Total current tax (credit)/charge	(23)	55

The Group had unrelieved UK corporation tax losses of approximately £7.5 m (2004: £11.3 m) at the end of the year.

The exceptional operating expenses of £2,369,000, representing the contractual amounts paid to former employees, reduce the deferred tax charge for the year by £0.7 m. The exceptional impairment expense reduces the deferred tax charge for the year by £0.9 m.

3. When tax authorities calculate the tax charge they do not base this calculation on the accounting 'profit before taxation' figure shown on the face of the profit and loss account. Some of the differences between accounting and tax treatment are permanent and simply have to be accepted with a shrug of the shoulders but others are temporary differences that should reverse out over time.

Deferred taxation = Tax on temporary differences

When preparing financial statements an approach called 'full provisioning' is used for temporary differences. This means that the future tax consequences of decisions taken today are reflected for the reader to assimilate.

The things every manager must know

1. Related party disclosures ensure that parties over whom control or influence are exercised, and the transactions that occur between them, are highlighted. This is important as in the absence of such disclosures a reader of the financial statements would assume that all transactions have been dictated exclusively by market factors.
2. The tax charge shown within the profit and loss account will rarely be a straight proportion of the profit before taxation. It is impacted by recognition of deferred taxation, profit estimation and the carry forward of tax losses from previous periods.

Group Financial Statements – The Basics

Problems associated with the veil of incorporation

The veil of incorporation refers to the fact that a company is a separate legal entity and hence the assets and liabilities reflected on its balance sheet are owned or owed in the name of the company and not its shareholders. The latter ultimately have the right to receive the value of the net assets upon the winding up of the business, but do not have title to the individual assets themselves.

When one company invests in the shares of another such that it gains control over its financing and operating decisions this creates significant problems for the shareholders of the investor company when trying to understand the nature of the investment (Figure 21.1).

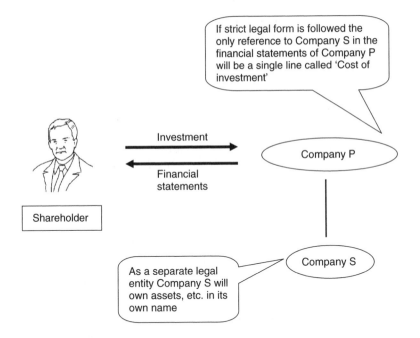

Figure 21.1 Strict adherence to the veil of incorporation

When the shareholders of Company P receive the financial statements they will know what the investment in Company S cost, but have no idea of the assets and liabilities of which it is comprised. Most would find this unacceptable given that they are the ultimate beneficiaries of Company P's net assets and yet have no idea of their true composition.

Commercial substance prevails again

You will recall from our earlier review of leasing that commercial substance is allowed to prevail over legal form to ensure that a reader of the financial statements is given a true and fair view. This concept is now applied again to alleviate the difficulties caused by the veil of incorporation.

The result is known as group or consolidated financial statements wherein the cost of the investment in a subsidiary company (i.e. one controlled by another) is replaced by its net assets on a line by line basis. A similar line by line approach is also adopted for the profit and loss account.

This is known as the *Single Entity* concept. In substance the two companies are viewed as a single entity ensuring that the recipients of the group financial statements are not prevented from seeing the assets and liabilities that lie within the entities the parent company has acquired.

A summary to the basic approach of preparing consolidated figures in the year when a subsidiary is acquired would be:

1. At the date of acquisition value all the assets and liabilities of the target company to their fair value, thereby allowing the consideration given for goodwill to be identified.
2. Add all the assets and liabilities of the target company to those of the parent on a line by line basis, and bring in the purchased goodwill as an intangible asset.
3. The 'Cost of Investment' line in the individual balance sheet of the parent company is eliminated as it has been replaced by the individual assets and liabilities. If retained this would effectively lead to double-counting.
4. Eliminate inter-company balances and inter-company trading. These have occurred within the single entity giving a zero net effect when viewed from outside. If they are allowed to remain the grossed-up figures would give a distorted view of the financial position and performance of the group.
5. Within the group profit and loss account the results of the subsidiary are only included from the date of acquisition and not for the whole year.

The logic for the treatment described above is that the parent company controls the assets of the subsidiary, but there appears to be one major flaw in our strategy! Control of a company can be obtained without owning 100 per cent of its shares, and we need to reflect this in the group accounts.

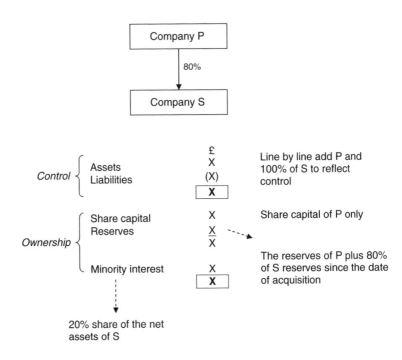

Figure 21.2 Consolidated balance-sheet proforma

NOTE: Looking at Figure 21.2 you might be asking what has happened to the share capital of Company S and the reserves it had generated prior to acquisition. These have been eliminated against the cost of investment line with Company P's individual books thereby allowing the balance sheet to balance.

Gaining control

The most likely way for one company to gain control over another is for it to acquire a majority of the ordinary (i.e. voting) share capital, but there are other mechanisms. These would include:

◆ It is a member (i.e. shareholder) and has the right to appoint or remove directors holding a majority of the voting rights

◆ It is a member and acts in concert with others
◆ It has the right to exercise control – this is an anti-avoidance measure whereby a company might have the power to exercise control but by electing not to use it could avoid the requirement to prepare group financial statements.

Influence only

If one company has influence over another a method is needed to reflect that this is a half-way house. Although full control cannot be exercised an investor in the parent company would want to know that some influence could be exerted.

Under these circumstances a method of group account preparation known as 'equity accounting' is used and the investment is referred to as an 'associate'.

Equity accounting requires the investment to be shown as a single entry in the balance sheet, but unlike a simple trade investment over which neither control-or influence can be exerted the associate is not shown at cost. Instead it is recorded as the parent company's percentage of the fair value of the associate's net assets plus any unimpaired goodwill arising on the acquisition. This single entry would be shown as a long-term investment.

Influence can normally be acquired through a 20–50 per cent stake in the ordinary share capital.

The things every manager must know

1. Group accounts are a further example of commercial substance prevailing over legal form.
2. When an investment is controlled by the parent company it will be referred to as a 'subsidiary'.
3. In the individual balance sheet of the parent company all investments (subsidiaries, associates trade investments, etc.) will be shown at cost.
4. In the group financial statements a subsidiary is consolidated on a line-by-line basis. This involves adding 100 per cent of the subsidiary's assets and liabilities to those of the parent to reflect

control, but separately disclosing those that are not owned as a minority interest.

5. When a parent can exercise influence over an investment it is designated as an 'associate and equity accounting' used in the preparation of the group accounts.

Putting your Skills to Use

The financial guru is born!

As we approach the end of our journey to understand the story told by financial statements it is worth reflecting on the ground covered.

We have looked at the mechanism by which commercial transactions are captured and incorporated within accounts, and it is important to emphasize that this is a common discipline to any financial information prepared around the World.

Tools have been developed, both qualitative and quantitative, to analyse the financial information presented to us, and we have considered the implications of the results for our ability to both understand the past and predict the future.

Accounting policies have been examined highlighting areas of choice, and also consideration given to some of the key areas where international accounting practice varies.

To complete our skill set all we need is a matrix into which these skills can be incorporated so that we adopt a systematic and thorough approach when those financial or management accounts land on our desk.

A systematic approach

Step 1

Make sure you know the objective!

There must be a reason for you being asked to review this financial information.

Step 2

If the financial statements have been subject to audit review the auditors' report. Have they qualified their opinion indicating that they disagree with the numbers? Qualifications such as this are rare for larger companies and their existence would immediately put us on guard.

Step 3

Read the financial statements in reverse starting with the notes and only then concentrate on the balance sheet, profit and loss account and so on.

This is an excellent approach to avoid being lulled into a false sense of security. It will force you to ask questions about what you expect the key documents to show instead of using the notes as an easy way to justify the numbers they support. If debtors have increased dramatically you will have asked yourself why rather than having the easy escape of simply turning to the note analysis.

Step 4

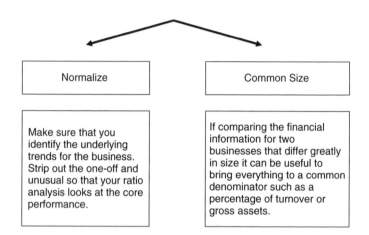

Normalize	Common Size
Make sure that you identify the underlying trends for the business. Strip out the one-off and unusual so that your ratio analysis looks at the core performance.	If comparing the financial information for two businesses that differ greatly in size it can be useful to bring everything to a common denominator such as a percentage of turnover or gross assets.

Step 5

Develop filters that are useful for the business sector you are reviewing to highlight figures that fall outside the expected range.

Filters could be taxation as a percentage of profit or movements in provisions/contingencies in the light of known changes to legislation.

Step 6

Calculate your ratios but try to use them as a surgical tool rather than a broadsword. Steps 1 to 5 should mean that you have already identified your priorities.

Step 7

Before asking any questions read the other information released with the numbers such as a directors' report or an operating and financial review as these might provide some of the answers.

Step 8

You are now ready to spring into action asking incisive questions and adding value to the conversation rather than being a passive observer.

The things every manager must know

1. For the non-accountant dealing with financial information is often perceived as a daunting task best avoided. Do not fall into this trap as a good grasp of the principles involved opens the doorway to a business story, and once conquered you will never look back!

Index